P9-DDX-320

CITY STREETS CITY PEOPLE

**A
Call for
Compassion**

CITY STREETS CITY PEOPLE

Michael J. Christensen

ABINGDON PRESS
Nashville

City Streets, City People: A Call for Compassion

Copyright © 1988 by Abingdon Press

All rights reserved.
No part of this work may be reproduced or transmitted in any
form or by any means, electronic or mechanical, including
photocopying and recording, or by any information storage or
retrieval system, except as may be expressly permitted by the
1976 Copyright Act or in writing from the publisher. Requests
for permission should be addressed in writing to Abingdon
Press, 201 Eighth Avenue South, Nashville, TN 37202.

This book is printed on acid-free paper.

Library of Congress Cataloging-in-Publication Data

Christensen, Michael J.
  City streets, city people : a call for compassion / Michael J.
Christensen.
    p. cm.
  Includes index.
  ISBN 0-687-08395-8 (alk. paper)
  1. City churches. 2. Church work. I. Title.
BV637.C46 1988   88-22216
253'.09173'2—dc19   CIP

ISBN 0-687-08395-8

"LITTLE CHURCH"—copyright © 1973 & 1974 by Famous Music
corporation.

Scripture quotations unless otherwise marked are taken from the
Holy Bible: New International Version. Copyright © 1973, 1978, 1984
by the International Bible Society. Used by permission of Zondervan
Bible Publishers.

Scripture quotations marked RSV are from the Revised Standard
Version of the Bible, copyright 1946, 1952, 1971 by the Division of
Christian Education of the National Council of Churches of Christ in
the USA. Used by permission.

Scripture quotations marked TLB are from *The Living Bible,*
copyright © 1971 by Tyndale House Publishers, Wheaton, IL. Used by
permission.

Manufactured by the Parthenon Press at
Nashville, Tennessee, United States of America

CONTENTS

LINCOLN CHRISTIAN COLLEGE AND SEMINARY

80492

FOREWORDS

I first met Michael Christensen in Haiti. I was a missionary and he was a young man on a pilgrimage. In many ways this book is the story of Michael's ongoing pilgrimage.

Since our first meeting, Michael has lived the experiences of ministry so clearly articulated in this book. I left Haiti to become my denomination's worldwide coordinator for Compassionate Ministries.

In my assignment, I travel our global village with the incredible mandate to offer hope where only despair is present. I encounter the world of extremes. The most visible of these extremes are those having to do with economics. I see starving children just a brief helicopter ride from an area filled with consumer abundance. But a more subtle extreme is how we are to respond to sin in our world. Some would have the entire Christian response centered on "stomachless souls." Others would, quite unintentionally, have us see eternal issues entirely in this world's physical dimension: "soulless stomachs." I pray daily that I truly will become one of the missionaries of Christ's love that Michael's book talks about.

City Streets, City People asks some pertinent questions, questions that must be answered. For example: Why has the conventional local congregation not adequately responded to the challenge of urban ministry? I found much insight and guidance in this volume to assist me in responding to the questions of how to practically engage in ministries of compassion.

While certainly not short on theology, this is not a theological volume. No, it is a practical guide to urban ministry. It reminds the reader of the need to personally engage in transformation ministries and gives bold and specific suggestions about how that practical engagement should take place.

This book is truly a must for anyone who is challenged to minister in the city but who lacks experience and background in this most demanding of all compassionate responses. Michael Christensen has experienced a love for urban peoples through a series of personal encounters. One can sense the struggles, the brokenness, the purging of motives—signs of his all-consuming involvement with the "losers" of our society.

Perhaps it is because I have walked city streets with Michael that the events and people he describes are so alive to me. Perhaps it is because this ministry, in this one city, in this one country, is so typical of God's prophetic witnesses whom I visit daily around our troubled and hurting world.

For some, the material will indeed become a guide to urban ministry. The six steps to building a community-based ministry will become literal steps to follow in developing a personal response to those in need.

Other readers will be made quite uncomfortable. Some of the underlying theological assumptions of the writer are in no way conventional. A book that addresses such subjects as our need for a theology that includes AIDS sufferers, advocacy issues, and the obvious maldistribution of God's resources, is asking for controversial response. But what is desired is dialogue, not argument. What is needed is ecclesiastical unity in response to suffering, not theological consensus, which will obviously not be part of this present level of existence in God's kingdom.

We who are called to minister (and who among us can claim to be exempt from this call?) must find our places on this spectrum of response to the suffering underclass. Each of us engaged in compassionate ministries must continually reevaluate our resources and our commitment to God's clear mandate of response to those who are the "least of these."

If God's people are going to make the difference in our world that Scripture clearly requires, then a new engagement in ministry will be necessary. This reengagement is symbolized by our response to the poor. Do we continue to be preoccupied with our ever-increasing affluence? Or do we engage in significant ministry that will directly affect our very existence as responsible consumers of God's resources?

God is clearly raising up his army of "compassionate volunteers." These front-line missionaries of Christ's love are doing their theology in the very center of sinful and fallen humanity. Whether God's people can regain their place as change agents and advocates for kingdom values is still an open question. But we will all be better equipped for our task by responding to God's call for compassion.

Steve Weber
International Coordinator
Compassionate Ministries
Church of the Nazarene

◆ ◆ ◆ ◆ ◆

My long years of ministry in the inner cities of America have led me to the conclusion that there is no substitute for superb role models. My brother and colleague Michael Christensen has provided such an example in his own life, and now in this user-friendly manual for inner-city ministry, *City Streets, City People.*

Having served as the founding chairman of the board of Golden Gate Ministries and having known and loved Michael since his freshman year in college—when he bounded into my life as a fervent but level-headed urban church volunteer—I have enjoyed a close-up view of this unique servant and his unique ministry. The book is for real, because the man is for real: a gifted thinker but a warmhearted lover of the poor and a devoted doer of the Word. His track record speaks for itself, and this book—which might be entitled *Everything You Always Wanted to Know About Launching Any Kind of Inner-city Ministry*—is based squarely on Golden Gate's proven work.

I heartily recommend this book. I heartily salute the man. I heartily embrace the ministry.

Paul Moore
Executive Director
Here's Life Inner City

PREFACE

Personal Pilgrimage in Urban Ministry

This year marks my fifteenth year in urban ministry. The journey has been one of youthful idealism, hard lessons in tough love, periodic burn-out and fresh new starts, fulfilled dreams and changed lives. Most important, it has been a journey with others on the same road of embracing *community*, *worship*, and *mission* in the city.

I was nineteen years of age and restless in the conservative, conventional church in which I was raised. Despite my rich and authentic evangelical heritage, I longed for something more. After growing up in a middle-class suburban home in Pasadena, California, the eldest son of a college professor, I decided to test the waters of urban ministry. The opportunity came through my pastor, Earl Lee, to spend a summer in New York City to help Paul Moore start an inner-city Nazarene church and mission. That summer of 1973 brought a wave of excitement and fulfillment that determined my life's direction. I dropped out of college for a while and served for a total of eight years as a "self-supported urban missionary" at the Lamb's mission in Times Square.

Idealistic about social action and helping the poor, I remember the first street alcoholic I encountered. He was lying in my path halfway in the street, with only his head and shoulders on the curb, near the corner of Forty-fourth Street and Eighth Avenue. With the compassion of innocence, I tried to rescue the man and tell him about Jesus. I picked him up, sat him against a building, and offered to buy him a hamburger and a cup of coffee. He only wanted money to buy another bottle of wine. I was amazed that an obviously hungry man didn't want food.

I had many such disappointments with the poor during that first year of ministry in the city. But I learned some valuable lessons. I lived in a seedy downtown hotel room, worked as a security guard at night, got to know the city, tried on different roles of ministry, and finally found my niche on staff coordinating gospel concerts, television coverage, and special events as part of our Christian witness in Times Square.

During that time I finished college and became associate pastor of the Lamb's Manhattan Church of the Nazarene. At twenty-five years of age, I had become an urban missionary and mass-media specialist in the city I had grown to love. But somehow along the way I got burned-out on helping the poor and living in Times Square. Slowly, my initial compassion had changed to academic interest in the poor and oppressed, and I had become detached from human need.

I retreated to Yale Divinity School where I was challenged by professors and students from a variety of religious traditions. I met Henri Nouwen, a Catholic priest and professor who taught intriguing courses on contemplative spirituality. He became a mentor, and I found myself attending the mass he led daily.

Liturgy, eucharist, and the rhythm of the church seasons were a new and wonderful balance to my "free church" background and Protestant upbringing. The more I read and studied about the early church, the desert fathers, the ancient mystics, and the devotional masters, the more I wanted to experience the monastic tradition that seemed to keep the Spirit of Christ alive all year round.

As graduation day approached, I became excited about a new assignment—starting a Nazarene church and mission in San Francisco. But before I could begin the new work, I wanted to spiritually prepare myself for what was ahead. I desired a monastic break before returning to active ministry. Professor Nouwen agreed: "Take some time simply to be in the Lord's presence," he told me. "Go to monastery and be quiet. Stop thinking so much about what you learned at Divinity School. Let your mind descend into your heart, and you will know what to do in San Francisco."

Graduation time came and went, and I checked myself into New Melleray Abbey in Iowa for forty days and nights. Having lived most of my life on the East and West coasts, the lonely cornfields of Iowa were a desert experience. I left the security of an Ivy League environment to embrace midwestern culture and solitude. The monastery was a foreign environment for a Nazarene urban minister. But what I gained there has been foundational for how I approach urban ministry today.

In the fall of 1981, I moved to San Francisco with five others to start the new work in the Haight Ashbury neighborhood. We all shared a common desire to be ecumenical in our community, worship, and mission, yet grounded in our Nazarene heritage. The exciting story of Golden Gate Community is presented in these pages, along with practical ways to accomplish compassionate ministry. What can be read between the lines is a philosophy of ministry that stems from a rich family heritage—a heritage of revivalism and social reform within the Holiness tradition.

The Holiness tradition in America began as a nineteenth and early twentieth-century movement among the economically poor and denominationally outcast, who experienced a baptism of the Holy Spirit subsequent to salvation and who sought to follow Christ in the tradition of John Wesley. It was a movement that brought both personal revival and social reform.

My father's parents were Holiness Mennonite missionaries to India in the 1920s and 1930s. They preached the gospel to the Hindus, built churches, and operated orphanages near Calcutta. On my mother's side, my great-great-grandmother was a Nazarene deaconess in wild West Texas. At the turn of the century, she preached to cowboys, held revival meetings, reached out to teenage prostitutes through street evangelism, and counseled unwed mothers at Cottage Rest Home in Pilot Point, Texas. In 1908, she became a charter member of the Church of the Nazarene.

As a fifth generation Nazarene, I am both proud of my heritage and concerned about my church's future commitment to compassionate ministry. In the early days, Holiness churches like the Church of the Nazarene successfully combined social action and the preaching of personal salvation. In 1895, our church founders, Phineas F. Bresee and his co-workers, went into downtown Los Angeles "feeling that food and clothing and shelter were the open doors to the hearts of the unsaved poor, and that through these doors we could bear to them the life of God."

The official minutes of the first meeting of the First Church of the Nazarene in Los Angeles, on October 30, 1895, read as follows:

We seek the simplicity and the power of the primitive New Testament church. The field of labor to which we feel called is in the neglected quarters of the cities and wherever else may be found waste places and souls seeking pardon and cleansing from sin. This work we aim to do through the agency of city missions, evangelistic services, house to house visitation, caring for the poor, comforting the dying. To this end we strive personally to walk with God and to invite others to do so.

Nazarenes at the turn of the century started street ministries, rescue missions, orphanages, hospitals, and homes for unwed mothers, as well as inner-city churches. It was Bresee's dream to have a place in the heart of every city "which could be made a center of holy fire, and where the gospel could be preached to the poor." To this end, he recommended that houses of worship be "plain and cheap" so that "everything should say welcome to the poor."

Historically, Nazarene churches attracted the poor and uneducated among the urban working class as well as rural farm laborers. Street people, orphans, widows, and neglected families were helped by members throughout the week and were entitled to a front-row seat in church on Sunday. The Church of the Nazarene took its name from the fact that Jesus was from Nazareth—a despised village filled with poor people so socially unacceptable that Nathanael initially said of Jesus, "Can anything good come out of Nazareth?" (John 1:46 RSV). According to the first piece of Nazarene literature ever published, the mission of the church was to preach the gospel to the poor "upon whom the battle of life has been sore."

As with other denominations, upward mobility, success, and institutionalization changed the urban focus and social witness of the Church of the Nazarene. White flight, church growth, and urban fear caused many churches to abandon the city and follow their members to the suburbs.

Today, however, we are seeing a dramatic return to compassionate ministry and a new "thrust to the cities"—to use the phrase of my denomination's renewed commitment to the urban mission field. Many churches are once again sending or supporting urban missionaries to operate soup kitchens, emergency shelters, group homes, and other kinds of compassionate ministry.

Other evangelical groups, especially charismatic ones, are fervently determined to redeem the cities for the Lord through service to the poor. Some liberal and mainline denominations are renewing their vision for urban ministry and seeing the need for spirituality as a basis for social action. The Roman Catholic Church, which never left the city and which has excelled in works of charity, also is enjoying a renewal in compassion and spirituality. It no longer surprises me to find a number of Catholics who are on the same journey of faith as I am—*a journey toward integrating contemplative spirituality, compassionate ministry, ecumenical community, and meaningful worship.* I am very proud to be part of an ecumenical network of churches in San Francisco joining together in cooperative ministry to feed, clothe, and shelter the homeless in Jesus' name.

As the church united responds to the biblical mandate to preach the gospel to the poor, as urban Christians rise to the challenge of *community, worship,* and *mission,* the signs of God's kingdom will become evident on city streets, among city people who need what the church alone can offer.

City Streets, City People celebrates God's work in the city. It calls for a revival of the historic mission of the church in neglected quarters of cities, as well as for starting new ministries among outcast and needy groups. It also shows how social action can be combined with the sharing of God's plan of salvation, resulting in biblical discipleship.

The challenge of urban ministry is the challenge to the church to adopt cities, where 80 percent of the world's population now lives, as its primary mission field. Urban ministry no longer is a novel undertaking by a select group of liberal social activists trying to "work out their salvation in fear and trembling." It now represents the most urgent item on the church's agenda, requiring specialized cross-cultural strategies and innovative approaches.

We are instructed in Scripture to seek the peace and welfare of the city where God has sent us, "for in its welfare you will find your welfare" (Jer. 29:7 RSV). If the peace and welfare of the city is one of God's chief concerns, and if God has sent us to the city to make a difference, we need a vision of God's kingdom in the streets. I hope my own pilgrimage will cast some light on the path that leads to peace.

Michael J. Christensen
San Francisco, California
Season of Lent, 1988

ACKNOWLEDGMENTS

I wanted to write a book on contemplative spirituality. My Abingdon editor, Michael Lawrence, challenged me: "First write a down-to-earth guide to urban ministry. In your next book, you can soar with eagles." For Michael's wisdom, support, and editorial direction, I am grateful.

Ten years ago Mary Ruth Howes and James Rutz edited my first book, *C. S. Lewis on Scripture* (Word, 1979). Both of them also were involved in the development of this project, Mary Ruth with her sagacious suggestions, Jim with his harsh green pen. Again, I am indebted.

Members and friends of Golden Gate Community— especially Steve Worthington, Jim Haynes, Paul Moore, Steve and Susan Gamboa-Eastman, and Mike and Brenda Davis—read chapters, offered critiques and shaped its development. I would not have finished without them.

Finally, to my wife, Rebecca J. Laird, my partner in life and ministry, who suggested the title and encouraged my creative process, I dedicate this publication.

1

BLESSED ARE THE LOSERS
A Biblical Basis for Urban Ministry

It is not the healthy who need a doctor, but the sick. . . . I have not come to call the righteous, but sinners. —Matthew 9:12-13

Benjamin, at eighteen years old street wise and fancy-free, with a criminal record a mile long, was a "throw away" youth—one of thousands of homeless persons on city streets across the nation. Rejected by his family for being a problem child, imprisoned by society for theft and attempted murder, Benjamin was a walking time bomb ready to blow when he got out of jail.

He was raised in San Francisco's infamous Haight Ashbury district in the 1960s; his father was a member of the Hell's Angels and his mother ran a hippie commune. "It was a rare day," Benjamin recalls, "when I wasn't beaten."

"I became a survivor, capable of anything, willing to break any law or rule that threatened my survival. I've been a street warrior, a burglar, a con, a hustler. I've

been in and out of foster homes, group homes, state and county institutions since I was six years old.

"I've lived on the streets, in the park, in vacant buildings, and in the attic of the house next door to the mission.

"In the past my idea of Christians was that they were a bunch of hypocrites. But after a while my ideas began to change."

Golden Gate Community members had befriended the lesbian couple who rented the house next door where Benjamin was staying. The entire household was invited over for meals and hospitality. Benjamin dropped by often just to talk and try to figure us out.

The first time Benjamin came to our church service was on Easter Sunday. He seemed to enjoy the informality of a house church, offered a critique of the service, and stayed afterward to help cook our Easter Agape Feast.

Later that night, he knocked on our door, and with simple brokenness and sincerity, surrendered: "You win; how do I become a Christian?" We prayed with him for forgiveness and the gift of faith, and the outcast pilgrim became a child of God. For the next five years, he slowly but surely found his way from the despair of street survival to new life in Jesus Christ.

"Knowing who and what I was, the community accepted me without question. They gave me friendship, trust, love, and support. They loaned me over $200 to help me rent an apartment. They even gave me the clothes I'm wearing now. And last but not least, they helped me find my way to Jesus Christ and continued to teach me about his life and word."

Shortly after his conversion, Benjamin was baptized in the Pacific Ocean. Nine months later, he suffered a setback and returned to being a "street tough."

He was allowed to continue coming to Bible studies for a while, as long as he checked his handgun at the door. Finally, in a spirit of "tough love," we excom-

22

municated him from the community until he could live
without his weapons and street identity. It was two
more years before he won the battle that had been
raging inside over who would control his life.

In a letter to the community dated November 18,
1984, Benjamin writes: "The Lord told me the road to
his presence was narrow and rock strewn. And so it
was. The times of frustration and failure far outnum-
bered those of success, and if the times I thought of
quitting were pennies, I'd be a millionaire. But again,
true to his word, when the night was darkest, the pit
deepest, he was there to carry me through."

"Since that day, I've been able to clean myself up,
physically as well as spiritually. I passed the G.E.D.
(high school equivalency exam), stopped smoking, and
began a more serious search for Christ, a search that
has led me on a 2,100-mile hitchhiking tour of most of
the western U.S. A search that has led me to apply for
admission to Northwest Nazarene College."

Benjamin was accepted and attended Northwest
Nazarene College in 1984. Although it was tough for a
street Christian to adjust to middle-class, suburban
Christianity in Idaho, it was there he met his future
wife, Rosalind. The two were married in San Francisco's Golden Gate Park in the presence of God and
the members of Golden Gate Community. They now
live in Oregon, have bought their own home, and have
a wonderful son, David. A second child is on the way.
Life is still a struggle, but the cycle of poverty and
violence has been broken. Their lives are examples of
God's power to transform.

Benjamin found the help he needed from a group of
Christians who lived in community and had formed a
house church and mission center to serve their
neighborhood.

Benjamin's testimony of finding a place where he

could fit in and offer his gifts and of overcoming street life and violence points to a growing need for church-type missions like Golden Gate Community that specialize in compassionate ministries.

Why has the conventional parish not met the challenge of urban ministry? Because by and large, it no longer favors the poor and oppressed or knows how to deal with troubled and homeless street people like Benjamin. White flight and urban fear caused many churches to abandon the city and follow their members to the suburbs.

Success, it seems, has spoiled the church and widened the gap between the rich and the poor, the secure and the outcast. In the process of upward mobility, the church often forgets her lowly origins and fails to continue preaching the gospel to the poor. Instead of providing facilities in locations where the poor feel at home, churches move to safer, more respectable neighborhoods, build bigger buildings, and attract more prosperous parishioners.

In an age of mainline and evangelical affluence, suburban church growth, and the rise of a success ethic, the church's ability to reach and include the down-and-out has been crippled. The poor no longer feel welcomed in our churches, and an urban crisis is at hand.

There is always a place in the church for the winners, but what about the so-called losers of the world, who may never taste success and affluence? Where are they to fit in? Does the church have anything to offer the abused child, the troubled young runaway, or the traumatized adult with destructive tendencies who ends up on the streets? Does the church have a word of hope for the down-and-out, the poor and oppressed, the orphans and pilgrims who are to be found everywhere, but especially in the city?

To respond to this urban crisis and challenge, let us take some time to focus on winning and losing in life's game, to assert the truth that God takes sides, to affirm

24

the biblical mandate for God's special interest in the poor, to consider the mission agenda of Jesus, and to sound the call to the urban mission field. This analysis will provide a theological foundation for a practical guide to urban ministry, which is what this book is about.

Winning and Losing

In life, some win and others lose. Winners are those with certain advantages, who get good breaks, succeed in reaching their goals, and come out on top. Losers are those with certain disadvantages, who think the cards are stacked against them, fail to advance, and end up at the bottom.

The determining factors in winning and losing are many. They begin, perhaps, with prenatal influences and early childhood experiences. A mother's drug addiction, a father's abuse, neglect or deprivation of love, can determine a person's identity and orientation to life. Whether one was the first or the last chosen for a school baseball game, for example, can make one feel like a success or a failure all one's life.

Choices, character development, and *chance* affect the winning and losing game. The sun of divine providence shines on the just and the unjust, and the rain falls on good and bad alike (Matt. 5:45). If the writer of Ecclesiastes is to be believed, the swiftest person does not always win the race nor the strongest person the battle. The good do not always have food to eat nor do wealth and favor come automatically to the wise, "but time and chance happen to them all" (Eccles. 9:11).

We do, of course, make choices in how we respond to personal circumstances. An ambitious and hard-working person can gain material comforts. A disciplined mind can be educated. A careful diet can improve one's health. Yet only a few overcome habit patterns and the lot they are dealt in life. When that happens, it is something like a miracle of deliverance.

Personal sin and social evil also account for why some win and others lose in the struggle of existence. Deprived of original blessing, human beings in their fallen state suffer both from a deceitful heart and an exploitative society. The human race is tainted with a compulsion that makes it easier to sin than to do the right.

Through a creative combination, then, of heredity, environment, chance, choice, and sinful nature, we are what we are in character and circumstances. The result in life is a division between the so-called winners and losers.

The essential question to ask in the winning and losing game is not "Why me, Lord?" but "Where are you, Lord? Whose side are you on?" Scripture's answer to the question reveals God's preference.

God Takes Sides

The longer I live in the city and the more I visit Third World countries, the more acutely aware I am of the truth that God has a special interest in certain groups of people, that is, those who are losers in the world's eyes, "least" in the sight of the church but greatest in the kingdom of heaven (Luke 9:46-48).

We live in a sinful, fallen world of pain and suffering. Everywhere we see abused children, mentally and spiritually broken men and women, social and economic outcasts desperate for acceptance and a word of hope. "Blessed are you poor," Jesus said to those listening to his sermon on the plain. The kingdom of God belongs to those who hunger, weep, feel excluded, and are persecuted unjustly (Luke 6:20-26).

But is not the kingdom of God for everyone, the rich as well as the poor, the powerful as well as the oppressed? The biblical answer is an unqualified yes. God loves all people regardless of circumstance and has a place for all in the kingdom. But this is not the issue. The core issue is whose side God is on in the struggle for existence. And the biblical answer is that God has a preference for losers!

World history is one long tale of class distinctions, racial conflicts, exploitation of the weak by the strong, and class struggles for dominance. God looks down in anger upon the arena of human struggle and is not impartial. God takes sides. And the side he takes is the side of the poor and the oppressed, the downtrodden and the hopeless, the outcasts and the underdogs of the world. God identifies not with the winners but with the losers.

Does this mean that God, as liberation theology teaches, is biased in favor of the poor and against the rich? Not exactly. The Scriptures reveal a God who ultimately is no respecter of persons (Deut. 10:17). God has the same loving concern for the rich as he has for the poor, for the great as for the small.

But in contrast with how the world treats the weak and disadvantaged, it *seems* as though God has favorites. It is precisely because God is no respecter of persons that God takes a special interest in those who are treated unfairly and need his help the most. For the sake of countering injustice, narrowing the gap between the rich and the poor, and making peace between the weak and the strong, God must take sides. Blessed indeed are the losers—orphans, widows, pilgrims, and the despised, afflicted, and impoverished—for the kingdom of God belongs to them.

A Biblical Mandate

God's heart has always been with the underdog—with people who cry out for deliverance, justice, equity, and peace. God's record of compassion is clear throughout biblical history, and so is the mandate for those who would be called children of God. Consider four strands of biblical teaching that reveal God's concern for the poor and oppressed and the implications of this for urban ministry.

1. Deliverance. God saw the affliction of the chosen people enslaved in Egypt, heard their cries, felt their pain, knew their suffering, and intervened (Exod. 3:7-8).

At crucial moments in human history, the Lord of the Universe is revealed as the Great Deliverer. At decisive moments of concern, God takes sides and "does not ignore the cry of the afflicted" (Ps. 9:12). When oppressed minorities, victims of mass violence, and the poor and needy cry out to God in their distress, God hears, God sees, and God delivers! How? Through God's people called to be advocates for those who need a Savior.

2. Justice. A second biblical mandate is God's concern for social justice. During a time of political security and economic prosperity, God sent Amos to the northern kingdom of Israel to condemn those who "oppress the poor and crush the needy" (Amos 4:1). He exposed the judges who deprived the poor of justice and took bribes (Amos 5:12). He called for social and economic justice in passionate words that were quoted three thousand years later by another prophet, the Reverend Martin Luther King, Jr.: "But let judgment run down as waters, and righteousness as a mighty stream" (Amos 5:24 KJV).

To those who seemed content with personal piety, the prophet Isaiah replied,

> Seek justice,
>   encourage the oppressed.
> Defend the cause of the fatherless,
>   plead the cause of the widow.
>
> (Isa. 1:17)

It is not enough to fast and pray inwardly. True spirituality is the expression of one's faith in action.

> Is not this the kind of fasting I have chosen:
>   to loose the chains of injustice
>   and untie the cords of the yoke,
>   to set the oppressed free
>   and break every yoke?
> Is it not to share your food with the hungry
>   and to provide the poor wanderer with shelter—
> when you see the naked, to clothe him,
>   and not to turn away from your own flesh and blood?"
>
> (Isa. 58:6-7)

3. Equity. A third strand of biblical teaching is that God desires equitable distribution of material resources. The widening gap between rich and poor is a contradiction of kingdom values and an abomination to God.

To reverse the natural process of the rich getting richer and the poor poorer, God delights in exalting the poor and humble and casting down the rich and proud. In the words of the Magnificat:

> He has brought down rulers from their thrones
>   but has lifted up the humble.
> He has filled the hungry with good things
>   but has sent the rich away empty.
>
> (Luke 1:52-53)

The biblical mandate for equity is not to be understood as demanding that everyone have exactly the same amount of money, land, possessions, or resources. Rather, equitable distribution means that no one has an abundance at the expense of those who have less than what they need. God desires equity, that the scripture might be fulfilled: "He that gathered much did not have too much, and he who gathered little did not have too little" (II Cor. 8:15, quoting Exod. 16:8).

4. Peace. Evangelical churches, more than mainline churches, have traditionally been out to "save souls" and "sanctify hearts." Biblically, what the church is to be about is the reconciliation of the whole person to the God of peace who sanctifies wholly (I Thess. 5:23). God is supremely concerned about the healing of the body, the cleansing of the soul, and the perfecting of the spirit in order to save the whole person from sin and dysfunction. The Old Testament simply uses one word to embody this truth: *shalom.*

Shalom is sometimes translated "peace," "prosperity," or "welfare." The concept points to the abundant life of joy, fullness, health, blessing, and friendship with God. *Shalom* means to be physically well, emotionally sound, and spiritually whole. The purpose of ministry in the city is to bring peace and wholeness to people's lives.

Jeremiah prophesied to the exiles in Babylon, "Seek the peace and prosperity of the city to which I have carried you into exile. Pray to the LORD for it, because if it prospers, you too will prosper" (Jer. 29:7). "Seek the *shalom* of the city" is the word of the Lord for urban Christians today. For in its *shalom,* you will find your *shalom!*

"In seeking the welfare of the city," writes George Webber, "pilgrims pray that they might be signs of shalom, hints of God's kingdom, the first fruits of God's promises." One way to view the role of the church is as a community of exiles and pilgrims, en route to the city of God. As we journey in faith, our ministry is to witness to the *shalom* that is available here and now. Webber continues: "Where there is hunger—seeking to feed, where there is sickness—seeking to heal, where there is loneliness—offering our love without any ulterior motive."[1]

The biblical concepts of deliverance, justice, equity, and peace offer a clear mandate of God's concern for the welfare of the socially disinherited of the earth. We turn now to the person of Jesus to see how this compassionate regard is personified in him.

The Agenda of Jesus

In a poor and obscure village, Jesus was born in a barn. His first visitors were shepherds, people of the land despised as outlaws by Jewish society. His poor parents were unable to bring the normal sacrifice to the temple. Instead of offering a lamb, they brought pigeons and prayed that their humble gift would be acceptable to God.

Threatened by the government, Jesus' family became refugees in Egypt (Matt. 2:13-15). Finally returning to Galilee, they settled in Nazareth, where Jesus studied the Scriptures and "grew in wisdom and stature, and in favor with God and men" (Luke 2:52).

Christians believe that God is revealed most completely in Jesus of Nazareth, the carpenter's son. How did the Incarnate One define his mission? What is the gospel according to Jesus? The answer is found in his first sermon.

Strategically, as if he were running for some political office, Jesus when he turned thirty returned to his hometown to announce his mission agenda and officially begin his public ministry. On the Sabbath day he went to the synagogue "as was his custom" (Luke 4:16). In the company of those who knew him best, he stood up to read the scripture that was handed him. Unrolling the scroll of Isaiah, he read where it is written:

The Spirit of the Sovereign LORD is on me,
  because the LORD has anointed me
  to preach good news to the poor.
He has sent me to bind up the brokenhearted,
  to proclaim freedom for the captives
  and release from darkness for the prisoners,
to proclaim the year of the LORD's favor.

(Isa. 61:1-2)

31

Then he rolled up the scroll, gave it back to the attendant, and sat down in the rabbinic chair to teach. Everyone's eyes were fastened upon him. Knowing he was Joseph's son, they were amazed at the simple dignity, authority, and confidence he displayed in saying, "Today this scripture is fulfilled in your hearing" (Luke 4:21).

Although some see only the spiritual dimension of Jesus' proclamation, in its first-century setting he was unquestionably referring to a class called "the poor." The poor were those who were economically destitute, socially oppressed, or spiritually impoverished. The brokenhearted and imprisoned were those who were physically, emotionally, and spiritually suffering in captivity. The mission agenda of Jesus was to exalt the "poor," release prisoners, heal the sick and blind, liberate the oppressed, and proclaim that the Lord is on their side with favor.

"The year of the Lord's favor" is a reference to Jubilee—a cyclical occurrence in Israel's history when God's favor focused on the poor and oppressed. Every seventh year debts were to be cancelled and slaves were to be set free. Every seventh Sabbath year—the fiftieth year, the year of Jubilee—poverty was to be alleviated and land was to be redistributed among the twelve tribes of Israel (Deut. 15:1-11; Lev. 25:23-24).

The significance of Jesus' inaugurating his ministry with a proclamation of Jubilee was that both spiritual and social transformation were being called for. His truly was a revolutionary agenda.

Certainly, Jesus came to show us how to be saved from the wrath to come, to open our blinded eyes, to soften our hard hearts, and to free us from spiritual bondage and guilt, as other texts show. But these truths are only part of the gospel. The good news of the kingdom, according to Jesus, is Jubilee—God is ready to pour out his favor on those who know themselves to be "poor"! The kingdom of God is proclaimed in Christ's coming, secured in his dying and rising, and carried forth by his disciples in living and bestowing the Lord's favor on people, until God's reign has finally come.

The mission agenda of Jesus was a liberating gospel with both social and spiritual implications, demanding radical discipleship and lifetime effort. It was both a proclamation of God's love and desire to save as well as a manifestation of God's love in acts of mercy and deliverance.

Jesus gained a reputation and a following for preaching to the poor, liberating captives, healing the sick, casting out demons, and encouraging the weak. He was the incarnation of God's heartfelt love for the poor and oppressed. The Pharisees accused Jesus of being a glutton and a drunkard, a friend of sinners, prostitutes, and tax collectors. To those who questioned why he ate, drank, and hung out with undesirables, he simply said, "It is not the healthy who need a doctor, but the sick. I have not come to call the righteous, but sinners to repentance" (Luke 5:31-32).

Jesus called all sinners to repent, but he also called the rich to serve the poor, the strong to be advocates of the weak, the righteous to live in such a way that their good works would glorify God. These were the terms of the kingdom.

The Urban Mission Field

Isaiah had a vision: When the Messiah came, the people of God would "repair the ruined cities, the devastations of many generations" (Isa. 61:4 RSV). The Messiah came, conquered sin and death, and began the process of restoration. The church, as the continuing incarnation of Christ in the world, has a messianic role to play in fulfilling the ancient vision. As God's chosen instrument of restoration, God is making his appeal through us (II Cor. 5:20). Our mission is to cooperate

33

with what God is doing in the world until the kingdom is fully come.

In the intensity of the personal needs and generational devastations of city people, the city is a strategic place for the coming kingdom. Urban ministry is the front line in the battle for the city's restoration and peace. The city means people, both winners and losers. God loves both, yet there is a special place in the divine heart for the Benjamins on the streets who wander into mission centers in need of a word of hope.

Blessed are the losers! The kingdom of God belongs to them. And blessed is the one who in God's name helps the poor, for the Lord will deliver him or her in time of trouble.

> The LORD will protect him and preserve his life;
>   he will bless him in the land
>   and not surrender him to the desire of his foes.
>
>   (Ps. 41:2)

Notes

1. George Webber, *Today's Church: A Community of Exiles and Pilgrims* (Nashville: Abingdon Press, 1979), pp. 93, 94.

2

COME TO KNOW YOUR POOR
The Different Faces of Poverty

Being unwanted is the greatest disease of all. This is the poverty we find around us here ... to be loved, to be someone. —Mother Teresa

Sometimes you must be confronted with poverty in another culture before you can recognize the face of poverty in yourself and in your own culture. This was true for me even after a decade in the city. Once I saw clearly the poor in the Third World, I came to recognize the poor in America. Similarly, when individuals and groups from the suburbs and rural areas come to visit the inner city, they go home with new eyes to see the poor in their own communities. "Come to know your poor" is the challenge of the gospel and the first step in urban ministry.

An Indian Pilgrimage

My grandparents were Christian missionaries in India in the 1920s and 1930s, and my father was born in Calcutta. I had had a growing desire since childhood to visit the orphanage my grandparents ran and see the city of my father's birth. My desire to experience India intensified upon hearing of Mother Teresa's work in the slums of West Bengal. In the summer of 1984, I found a way to visit Calcutta, work with the Missionaries of Charity, and learn from Mother Teresa's compassion in the city.

Calcutta is, I think, one of the most wretched cities in the world. For nine days I walked the streets in shock as I witnessed how ten million people struggle to survive. Everywhere I turned I was confronted with extreme disease and poverty: A half million sleep on the streets; thousands of the destitute on the threshold of death can be found near the train stations and under Howrah Bridge. Live infants are sometimes thrown into garbage cans, lepers are tossed into gutters, and aging parents rejected by their children are left to die alone.

Some of these rejected, disfigured, and diseased ones are rescued by a Missionary of Charity and brought to the malnutrition center for infants, the leper home, or the home for the dying. I volunteered for several days at these homes and offered what meager gifts I had. As a co-worker of Mother Teresa, I dispensed medicine, hand-fed those too weak to sit up to eat, massaged legs that were skin and bones, and assisted nurses trying to save lives.

What Mother Teresa says about compassionate ministry is this: "Being unwanted is the greatest disease of all. This is the poverty we find around us here. The hunger is not so much for bread and rice but to be loved, to be someone."[1]

In this intense setting, I learned that poverty has many faces, some less obvious than others. Poverty can have the face of an unwanted baby, an abused child, a runaway youth, a rejected spouse, a lonely old man, or an AIDS patient. Poverty can be physical, emotional, or spiritual. To be impoverished means to lack love and the essentials of life: food, clothing, shelter, health, support, identity, and purpose. The economically poor and the spiritually impoverished have the same basic need—to know that their welfare is God's concern.

Mother Teresa has spent a lifetime witnessing to the truth that we love God by loving God's poor. "And we must prove God's love, not by words but by actions," she says. "In order to love the poor, we must come to know the poor!"[2]

"Come to know your poor" is the challenge not just of Mother Teresa but of the Lord. If the poor in Calcutta are diseased lepers or dying outcasts, who are the poor in my neighborhood or yours? In my city of San Francisco, the poor are homeless families, persons with AIDS, new immigrants and refugees, runaway youths, and street people who live in the park near my home. In rural Yuba City where my brother and his family live, the poor may be rejected Sikhs, Asian immigrants, orphans and widows in the church, flood victims in the valley, or farmers who have lost their crops.

"Come to know your poor" begins with personal recognition of one's own needs and impoverishment. It is practiced at home in recognizing members of one's own family who feel unloved and have unmet needs. It extends into society in identifying persons who have been ignored as outcasts by the mainstream. In recognizing poverty wherever it is found, we can embrace it and transform it in Jesus' name.

Recognizing Personal Poverty

I was not prepared for India. Daily contact with the poor of Calcutta caused me initial discomfort, which gradually mirrored to me my own "dis-ease" and impoverishment. I was not as compassionate as I fancied myself, not as at peace with myself and others as I had believed. In fact, I had strong impulses to flee the presence of the poor, to "freak out" in the face of suffering, to become immobilized when requested to assist with a person who was dying.

I'll never forget the occasion when I discussed my feelings with Mother Teresa. Before working in the homes each day, 296 sisters and a dozen co-workers attend morning mass at 5:45 at the Mother House where the sisters live. After mass one morning, I confessed to Mother Teresa how I felt about working in her homes. "Did you see Jesus?" she asked me. I could not say a truthful yes because all I saw was suffering, disease, and death. I was simply trying to find the courage to expose myself to subhuman conditions and cope with my emotional shock.

Mother Teresa tried to help me see it from her perspective: "When we love the poor," she said, "we do not first see the poor; we first see Jesus! We are not social workers but missionaries of Christ's love. We do it for Jesus! And when we pick a body off the street and nurture him back to health, we do it to Jesus! It is His face we see in the faces of the poorest of the poor."

As we sat on a bench outside the chapel, Mother Teresa took my hands in hers and said, "The gospel is written on your fingers." She slowly pointed to each of my five fingers and said, carefully emphasizing each word, *"You–did–it–to–me."*

She brought my five fingers together and said, "See the five wounds of Jesus?" I thought about the two wounds in his hands, the two in his feet, and the one wound in his side. Putting my pointed fingers into the palm of her hand, she said softly: "This is His love for you."

"Now close your fist," she said. "This is the sacred heart of Jesus that says to us: 'When I was hungry, you gave me to eat; when I was thirsty you gave me drink; I was a stranger and you took me in, naked and you clothed me; I was sick and you visited me.'

"And at the end of life," she added, "your five fingers

will excuse you or accuse you of doing it unto the least of these. *'You–did–it–to–me!'* "³

I was overcome by the simple truth of the gospel from the mouth of Mother Teresa. "By their fruits you will know them," she was saying. But the truth hit home deeper than that. I was in the presence of someone who practiced personal poverty, and I was being broken in the process of sensing the humble spirit of Mother Teresa. Perhaps for the first time, I prayed for a "broken and contrite heart" that recognized its own spiritual poverty: "Hear, O LORD, and answer me, for I am poor and needy" (Ps. 86:1). What I experienced in the days that followed was a breakthrough in coming to know and love God's poor wherever they are found.

"Blessed are the poor in spirit," Jesus told his disciples, "for theirs is the kingdom of heaven" (Matt. 5:3). If heaven is for the spiritually poor, then what does this say to those of us who find it difficult to identify with those whom the Scriptures call "poor"? More personally, what does the Word of God say to Michael Christensen—who was born into a good, strong, healthy, educated, and comparatively well-off family, who has advantages and has succeeded in many things, and who has not suffered much in life?

On one level, the gospel confronts us all with the truth that unless you know yourself to be poor in spirit, in need of health and wholeness, there is no salvation for you. Only the sick need a doctor, and only poor sinners need a Savior.

On another level, the Lord meets us where we are with the challenge, "What are you doing for the least of mine?" Since God Almighty identifies with the poor and oppressed, so must we involve ourselves with those to whom justice has been denied and life has been cruel. In the same way that Christ emptied himself of his divine power and riches to become a humble servant (Phil. 2), so must we empty ourselves of our extravagances and successes and become servants of our fellow men and women.

Spiritual poverty simply means following the way of divine descent after Jesus Christ, who "though he was rich, yet for your sakes he became poor, so that you through his poverty might become rich" (II Cor. 8:9). Homeless Christians among us remind us of Jesus' humble words: "Foxes have holes and birds of the air have nests, but the Son of Man has no place to lay his head" (Matt. 8:20).

"Downward mobility" (simplicity) for the privileged classes is usually harder to achieve than "upward mobility" (success) is for the underclass. The rich have too much to lose and the poor everything to gain. As Christ said, "It is easier for a camel to go through the eye of a needle than for a rich man to enter the kingdom of God" (Matt. 19:24 RSV). A miracle of spiritual brokenness is required to embrace personal poverty, as well as to take the next important step.

Who Are the Poor in My Own Family?

In the spring of 1982, Mother Teresa addressed the graduating class at Harvard University. Few of the college seniors, I would imagine, had ever seen the face of poverty in the Third World, in the inner city, or even in themselves.

To these somewhat sheltered, elite students, the Missionary of Charity said, "Come to recognize the poor you have in your own family." What she meant was that compassion begins at home, first by knowing oneself as poor and needy, and then by acknowledging the needs for love and acceptance that one's parents, brothers and sisters, and other relatives feel. Unless one can understand them and learn to meet their needs, it is a mockery to say one knows and loves the world's poor.

Immediately, as I write these words and affirm them in my head, my heart finds it painful to acknowledge the poverty in my own family. My parents have had their share of suffering, to which I was not always present. My brothers have needs I know nothing about. I have an alcoholic relative who managed to recover without any help from me. I hope to be able to come through for my young gay cousin whose lover died of AIDS.

Paradoxically, or perhaps as overcompensation, it is easier to do something for society's poor than for the poor in one's own family.

Many inner-city social activists and world pilgrims of solidarity suffer from estranged relationships at home. Unable to love and be reconciled to wife, husband, father, mother, they live out their lives doing unconscious penance. In trying to love and serve the poor without dealing with their broken family relationships, they develop subtle attitudes of superiority, condescension, and ungenuine compassion.

One of my social activist acquaintances, John, is a not uncommon example of this complex: At forty years of age, he has lived in Africa, Bangladesh, Central America, Los Angeles, and San Francisco in solidarity with the poor. Bright, articulate, and competent, John has organized relief and development programs, mediated migrant farm workers' disputes, instigated non-violent political action, and called attention to the needs of the homeless.

By all appearances, John comes across as a compassionate servant of the Lord, and he is! But underneath the surface is a well of hidden needs, unreconciled relationships, and unresolved conflicts that he cannot face. If he would honestly face his own personal poverty and the impoverished relationships within his family, John could embrace the world's poor from a position of spiritual strength rather than from one of hidden weakness. "Wounded healers" can only heal others' wounds as they offer to God their own.

Understanding Society's Poor

Visiting Calcutta and meeting Mother Teresa helped me recognize the face of poverty not only in myself and in my family, but also in my own neighborhood. In San Francisco's Haight Ashbury, where I live and work, there is malnourishment, but not starvation. There is homelessness, but few freeze to death. The needs in the Haight do not seem as intense and obvious as in Calcutta, or even as in Chicago or New York City. Yet when I look in people's eyes and see pain and despair, I see the poor whom God loves and I must come to know.

Jeffrey, twenty-four, sleeps in the park under a clump of trees across the street from our mission center. He admits to being unwanted since the age of seven, when his mother died. His wealthy father tried to raise him alone, but, eventually committed him to a mental institution. After unsuccessful treatment for manic depression, Jeff became a drifter and drug addict in search of family, purpose, and a place to call home.

Several factors contribute to poverty and homelessness in America, including growing up unwanted, broken families, mental illness, displacement, substance abuse, lack of education and basic life skills, spiritual chaos, and personal choice. Jeff seemed to suffer from them all when we first met him.

To come to know the homeless poor, Golden Gate Community hosted hospitality times each evening for people like Jeff, who needed to come in out of the cold, relax for an hour, enjoy a snack, get some clothes, and talk about God.

In the interest of understanding the backgrounds and needs of those we served, we took a survey one winter, asking 168 street folks to fill out a profile sheet. Jeff, who had moved from the park to a squat under a vacant house and who volunteered every day at the mission, compiled the survey results.

Eighty-one percent of those surveyed were single men, eighteen to thirty-nine years of age. The majority of these had no source of income and were unemployed. Thirty-three percent had finished high school, and 41 percent had electrical, construction, or general labor experience. Although 60 percent said they had no religious affiliation or background, 18 percent identified their tradition as mainline Protestant, 10 percent as evangelical/fundamentalist, and 8 percent as Roman Catholic. Sixteen percent admitted to being a current drug user. And 13 percent identified their support group as Alcoholics Anonymous, while 7 percent claimed a support group in their church.

What we learned from this survey and from daily encounters with our guests is that the poor of Haight Ashbury belong to a larger class of people in America who slip through the cracks of the social system and are deemed unlikely to ever get out from under the circumstances that keep them poor and oppressed. How are we to love those who feel hostile toward the mainstream or are unable to advance? The answer is "to love the poor you must come to know the poor," through sociological study and personal encounter.

The Underclass: A Sociological Study

There have always been beggars, vagrants, paupers, disadvantaged, disabled and dependent individuals. These and a new wave of poor and homeless families now form a new and distinct social class. They often come from middle-class homes but they soon get stuck at the bottom with the generational poor.

In New York's Times Square, a pretty, blond-haired girl in satin hot pants, heels, and a tight tapered blouse stands under the bright lights of a theater marquee on Forty-fourth Street and Broadway. Her name is Suzy; she's sixteen, from Tennessee. Her story is similar to that of many of New York's twenty thousand teenage prostitutes who end up on the streets: "My daddy beat me and I decided to run. Caught a bus for Port Authority. Didn't know anyone in town; found a friend who turned out to be a pimp. Sometimes I want out, but I don't know, could be worse . . ."

In Chicago's North Side, legal and illegal refugees crowd inside a church, hoping to get some food from a pantry. One of the recipients is Mr. Lee from Cambodia, who has to feed his family of seven. The church had sponsored him when he first arrived, and even found him a job. But life is difficult in a new country, and a little extra provisions go a long way.

In downtown Los Angeles, skid row alcoholics wander into a rescue mission that offers a free meal if they can sit through a church service. Russell, twenty-three, who only recently started drinking, finds someone who will listen to his story: "I had a family. I went to college. I held a job. But my daddy died and the money he left me was stolen from me cold. . . Can you spare some change for a bus ticket back to Mama?"

In Washington, D.C., not far from the White House, a black family of six is evicted from a dilapidated apartment complex. Police are literally throwing all of Mrs. Robinson's possessions onto the streets as the

*mother screams in disbelief, "What about my babies!
What about my babies!" The landlord coolly responds,
"If you can't pay the rent, then don't expect to live
here."*

Welcome to the world of the underclass. Real-life
examples serve to remind us that research statistics
have names and faces, hopes and dreams, problems and
needs that society largely ignores.

Research reveals that thirty million Americans fall
below the official poverty line. Of this group, there is a
chronic subculture of ten million Americans who are
not just economically poor but who remain stuck at the
bottom of the social ladder.

This non-working, unassimilated, hard-to-reach
marginal class is centered in cities and is referred to by
different names: the downtrodden, the underprivileged,
the disadvantaged, the down-and-out, outcasts, or
simply the "underclass."

Ken Auletta, a resident of New York City with eyes to
see and a heart to know, wrote an insightful book
entitled *The Underclass* about America's hard-core
poor who have succumbed to hostility and helplessness—to feelings of being out of control and unable to
advance.

Ten years ago *Time* magazine devoted its cover story
to the underclass on August 29, 1977. Since then there
have been countless television documentaries and
feature articles on the subject. My own experience and
reflection confirm a number of findings on this subject,
which I will attempt to summarize in this section.

Most members of the underclass are economically
poor as well as emotionally impoverished. Some of its
members include families with a long history of welfare
dependency, the chronically homeless, traumatized
alcoholics and drug addicts, bag ladies and derelicts,

ex-convicts and youth offenders, illiterate school dropouts, and released mental patients.

The underclass also includes violent gang members, male and female prostitutes, and street criminals who may not be economically poor.

The underclass is composed of people from all strata of society who lack the education, personality traits, life skills, personal discipline, and motivation needed to be effective and valuable in the world of work and responsible living. They cannot "pull themselves up by their bootstraps" because they simply don't know how. No one bothered to teach them, and they did not find role models.

The demographics of this subculture are significant. Although the majority are non-white (70 percent), growing numbers of whites also belong to this group. Fifty percent are from single mother households, 70 percent are under eighteen years of age, and 85 percent are male.

The values found among members of the underclass may seem surprising: Patriotism runs strong, just as it does in the mainstream; loyalty to friends and extended family is more important than honesty; survival instincts supersede all other values. Religious devotion is common.

In my own experience on the streets of San Francisco, for example, belief in God among the street people is so prevalent that one could easily sit and discuss religion all day. One church group in the city discovered a loosely knit band of homeless cave dwellers who live under the streets and hold prayer meetings underground. When taking them food, church members were surprised to see the subterranean squatters joining hands in prayer before meals and reading the Bible.[4]

In studying the behavior of the underclass, several generalities have been determined: Its members have a low tolerance for frustration, a pattern of surrendering to impulse and moment-to-moment living, difficulty sustaining relationships, a disorganized life and schedule, difficulty submitting to authority, and a lack of discipline and life skills.

"The most important factors in whether or not someone makes it," according to Auletta, "are drive, self-confidence, self-esteem, and the ability to wrestle with and control frustrations."[5] These winning characteristics do not come naturally but are the benefits of a secure family structure and of learning beneficial values.

According to the *Time* cover story on the underclass, "It is the weakness of the family structure, the presence of competing street values, and the lack of hope amidst affluence all around that make the American underclass unique among the world's poor peoples."[6]

If a person grows up in a broken family, with abusive parents, and in a negative environment of criticism, hostility, and dependency, these dynamics will repeat themselves in what is called the "cycle of poverty."

Lack of discipline and failure to learn life skills early in life make it nearly impossible to overcome inferiority and failure later in life. Prolonged poverty produces stress, temper outbursts, and vulnerability to emotional disorder. Physical and emotional abuse leads to repeated violence.

Disadvantage and inability to cope leads to escape from reality through drugs, alcohol, or fantasy. Dependent personalities manifest themselves in alcoholism, substance abuse, or sexual addiction. The street becomes a sanctuary for those who can no longer endure.

Does the church have a role to play in evangelizing and making disciples of those cut off from society and responsible living? Are members of the underclass unreachable or unresponsive to God's love? Can compassionate ministry make a difference? To love and help the poor, we must first come to know them, not just sociologically but through personal encounters. I want you to meet Richard, a member of the underclass.

A Portrait from the Gallery of Despair

"Unloved and unwanted" was how Richard felt about himself. He had problems that never seemed to go away. He suffered more than his fair share. He believed in God; he tried to have faith; he wanted to overcome his destructive habit patterns; he wanted to advance; but he never got it together. Yet God loves Richard just the way he is, and nothing can separate him from God's love!

Richard was born in 1948, to parents in Little Rock, Arkansas. His father was killed in Korea when Richard was three years old. Richard remembers his mother dying four years later "of a broken heart."

He lived with his Christian grandparents for a while, then with an uncle. Because he was a "problem child," Richard was shuffled from one institution to another, finally finding a foster home at age eleven.

He could never live up to his foster father's expectations, he remembers, and he rebelled. At eighteen he left home, and his "family" asked him never again to use their name.

Richard roamed up and down the California coast for many years as a drifter. He married a woman and was soon divorced; he became a Christian but couldn't live the life; he became a drug addict and couldn't stop using. Percodan and Valium were his drugs of choice.

To complicate matters, Richard had a seizure disorder that caused him to black out without warning. And he had hypoglycemia, which caused him to crave food and eat constantly.

He found doctors willing to supply and caseworkers willing to sympathize, and he managed to create a network to get the drugs and food he required. After he had exhausted his resources in Los Angeles, he appeared in San Francisco.

It was August 1981 when Susan Gamboa, a member of Golden Gate Community and a Salvation Army social worker, met Richard in her office. As his caseworker for a year, she gave him food vouchers each month and tried to help him manage his life.

Michael Dotson, former pastor and mission director at Golden Gate Community, picked up where Susan left off in September 1982. For the next three and a half years, Michael spent an average of three hours a week as Richard's payee (money manager), emotional supporter, confessor, and caseworker.

Michael secured housing for him from time to time, got him out of jail, and protected him when loan sharks were after him. Michael rebuked him for his alcohol and drug consumption, rewarded him when he was straight, encouraged him in personal hygiene, and kept him involved in church.

Richard stabilized a bit at Golden Gate Community. His happiest moment was when he was asked to be a church usher. Also, he happily developed an emotional attachment to Dulcie, twenty-four, a cancer patient and member of the congregation. (They used to play video games together after services.) When Dulcie died in 1985, Richard took it the hardest and never really recovered.

Ken Niles, our mission social worker and counselor, became Richard's therapist. For seven months he tried to help Richard deal with the loss of his parents, his foster father's rejection, the loss of his wife, and a lack of belonging. "He did drugs and drank to kill the pain and forget his childhood," Ken concluded.

Richard had his teeth pulled one by one to get more Percodan. He had a craving that nothing in life could

49

satisfy. He was drawn to God, wanted to join the church, but could never manage to attend membership classes or stay sober long enough to make a new commitment.

He disappeared for several months in 1986, and then came back to church in April. During one memorable service, Richard prayed for forgiveness. He died a month later.

After being a mission client and church attender for four years, at thirty-eight years of age, Richard was found dead in his room by a friend who told us: "His door was open and television on. He was kneeling over his bed facedown in a cup of blood."

Richard's friend suspected foul play. According to the police, who found an empty bottle of Percodan nearby, it was just another drug-related suicide in the city. "Percodan and cocaine poisoning" was the official cause of death, according to the coroner.

There was no obituary in the newspaper, no family to notify, and very few even cared. His memorial service was held at the Oak Street House, nine months after his death. It took a while for the city to cremate his body, determine if there were any relatives, and finally turn over the ashes to Golden Gate Community, the only family that knew him or wanted him.

Despite his pathetic, peripheral life, Richard had endeared himself to us. Many of us had talked him out of suicide now and then. We had forgiven him when he got angry and broke our window. We had welcomed him on Sunday mornings for church and during the week days for social services. Between Susan, Michael, and Ken alone, we had invested over five hundred hours of time and energy and undoubtedly had extended his life a few years.

The handful of people who journeyed with Richard or felt an affinity with him attended his memorial service in 1987. We buried Richard's ashes under a tree in front of the Oak Street House, in a colorful urn lovingly created by his counselor. One of our mission residents built a flower box around the memorial site.

Sister Linda, Richard's caseworker from St. Anthony's Kitchen who helped him acquire his birth certificate and who logged many hours of advocacy in his behalf, summed up her feelings this way: "He is surely in heaven now at rest, for he suffered so much in this life."

The scripture that was read at Richard's memorial service assures us that God's great love and mercy extends especially to those who live at the margin of life and never find its center: "For I am convinced that neither death nor life, neither angels nor demons, neither the present nor the future . . . will be able to separate us from the love of God that is in Christ Jesus our LORD" (Rom. 8:38).[7]

"Coming to know your poor" happens through a process of spiritual adoption and through extending community life to those who feel unloved and unwanted. There are people in every family, church, neighborhood, and city who doubt whether anyone really cares. Christians are called to take a special interest in those society neglects. Somehow, working out our salvation depends on coming to know and love God's poor.

Notes

1. Michael J. Christensen, "You Did It to Me," *Herald of Holiness* 173, no. 23 (December 1, 1984): 5.

2. Commencement speech at Harvard University, 1982.
3. Christensen, "You Did It to Me," p. 6.
4. "Invisible Homeless Find Refuge Under S.F. Streets," *San Francisco Chronicle*, December 15, 1986.
5. "A Closer Look at America's Hard-Core Poor," *San Francisco Chronicle*, May 26, 1982.
6. "The American Underclass," *Time* 110, no. 9 (August 29, 1977): 16.
7. Michael J. Christensen, "Nothing Can Separate Us from the Love of God," *Herald of Holiness* 77, no. 6 (March 15, 1988): 8-9. Used by permission of publisher.

3

LIFT UP YOUR EYES

How to Start an Urban Ministry

Show me your dreams, and I will show you your future.
—Dr. Paul Yongi Cho

The church needs visionaries who choose not to play it safe but to take risks and trust God in starting new and innovative ministries in the city.

I am grateful for the visionaries in my life—Earl Lee, Paul Moore, and Henri Nouwen—who have showed me the importance of discerning what God is doing and of becoming part of it (John 5:9).

God's will for many of us points to the city. If God has called you to the inner city to start something new, as God has me, then you will go through a process of discerning God's will, stepping out in faith, and building your dream.

The steps in discerning and starting new ministries are these: (1) Let the Spirit dream in you; (2) build your dream slowly; (3) recruit qualified co-workers; (4) adopt a neglected neighborhood; (5) secure an outpost; (6) build community; and (7) let mission flow. I offer my own experience in New York City and San Francisco as a pattern for others with dreams and visions to realize.

53

Step One: Let the Spirit Dream in You

God gives us glimpses of his plan and purpose for our lives and allows us to dream and envision clearly and concretely. The more specific our visionary prayers, goals, and objectives are, the more likely the vision is to be fulfilled.

A dream or vision is a picture burning in your heart of what God wants to do through you in a certain place with a specific group of people. Visions are revelations of what can happen. A unified nation of people living together in a land of promise, for example, is conceived as a vision mirroring the mind and heart of God. By believing and acting on the vision, the dream becomes reality. Two ancient visionaries, Abraham and Sarah, embody this truth. I see three threads in the fabric of their lives that form a present-day pattern for discerning God's will: a call to obedience, faith in the vision, and anticipated results.

The Call to Leave One's Homeland

Abraham and Sarah were secure and settled in Haran when God called them out: "Leave your country, your people and your father's household and go to the land I will show you" (Gen. 12:1). It was not easy for them to obey the call. It meant risk and sacrifice to venture into unknown territory. One does not venture in faith in comfortable surroundings, but in the desert.

A "call" is simply the still, small voice within you saying, "Leave the place where you are and go to where I show you." The place we leave may be geographical or spiritual. The place we are shown may be the city, a new ministry in our own backyard, or a new way of being in the world. The important thing is to respond and follow the vision that is born within us, regardless of the risk or sacrifice.

When Abraham and Sarah left familiar surroundings for the unknown, their nephew Lot went with them. A dispute arose between Abraham's and Lot's herdsmen over the division of land. Abraham, trusting in his vision, suggested that they part company: "If you go to the left, I'll go to the right; if you go to the right, I'll go to the left."

Lot looked East and "saw that the whole plain of the Jordan was well watered, like the garden of the Lord, like the land of Egypt." Based on immediate appearances, Lot chose for himself the lush Jordan plain and settled near Sodom. Abraham was left with the hilly country of Canaan that did not seem as pleasing to the eye. It was at the point of departure that God confirmed Abraham's vision: "Lift up your eyes from where you are and look north and south, east and west. All the land that you see I will give you and your offspring forever" (Gen. 13: 9-10, 14-15).

There is a lesson here for today's urban visionaries: *The eyes of faith do not focus on appearances but look up and visualize what can be.* "What you can see beyond the immediate, I can give you," God is saying to people of faith. "What you cannot envision, I cannot give you."

In 1973 a young, longhaired, rock-and-roll pastor by the name of Paul Moore had a vision of starting a Nazarene church and urban ministry in Manhattan, a city that had been neglected by his denomination for sixty-four years. Paul looked up from his impossible circumstances—no money, no staff, no building—and visualized what could be if he believed and acted on God's calling.

What could be was a new congregation of single young adults enthusiastic about their lives as Christians. What could be was a Christian theater company, a contemporary Christian band, a soup kitchen, a crisis care ministry, and a Christian community center in Times Square hosting creative ministries to the glory of God.

Paul shared his dream with my home church in Pasadena, California. The congregation responded by pledging $30,000 and sending eight volunteers to help start the new work. I was one of those who caught the vision and stepped forward.

When I left home to become part of the New York vision, I was nineteen years old. I had grown up in Pasadena, and had never lived in the big city. But the call was so clear and my desire so strong that I was willing to leave friends behind, delay my junior year of college, raise my own financial support, and take whatever risks were required to be an urban missionary.

There were a dozen of us from different parts of the country who had joined Paul and Sharon Moore in Manhattan. We rented a brownstone, lived and worked together, and held church services in the backyard on Sundays. Twice a week we shared our faith on the streets and in the singles' bars on the Upper East Side. On Friday nights we enjoyed Bible study together in the "upper room." On Saturdays we opened and hosted the Innerlight Gospel Café featuring our own gospel rock band, the Manhattan Project, and attracted new people to our fellowship. Our experience, we felt, was as fresh as that of the early believers in Jerusalem, who

> devoted themselves to the apostles' teaching and to the fellowship, to the breaking of bread and to prayer. Everyone was filled with awe, and many wonders and miraculous signs were done by the apostles. All the believers were together and had everything in common. Selling their possessions and goods, they gave to anyone as he had need. . . . And the Lord added to their number daily those who were being saved. (Acts 2:42-47)

Within two years of the birth of a church in Manhattan, we envisioned a building of our own in which to worship and minister. The Lambs Club was available in the heart of Times Square, a "red light" neighborhood that attracts New York City's homeless population as well as the artistic community that frequents performances at the many Broadway theaters.

Designed by Stanford White near the turn of the century, the landmark building housed the Lambs, America's oldest theatrical club whose members included Milton Berle and Spencer Tracy. In later years, however, dwindling membership and poor management forced the club into bankruptcy. Valued at $1.7 million, it was offered for a half million, a hefty sum even by New York standards in the early 1970s.

The six-story facility, which included a four hundred seat auditorium, thirty-five residency rooms, a grill room designed like an English pub, expansive office space, and a restaurant-sized kitchen and ballroom, seemed ideal for a church and community center.

The congregation that had grown to one hundred prayerfully asked the Lord for a building and a ministry so far beyond its own means, that unless the project was in God's will, it could not happen. Pastor Moore challenged us with the story of Abraham to trust God for the otherwise impossible. Abraham looked up, opened his spiritual eyes, and walked through the length and breadth of the land God had promised him. He was able to envision his descendants as numerous as the grains of sand of the earth (Gen. 13:16). Under a clear, starlit sky, God confirmed the vision: "Look at the heavens and count the stars. . . . So shall your offspring be" (Gen. 15:1-5).

"Lift up your eyes and visualize" is the key to results beyond our human resources. If we can dream God's dream and be specific about the results, what we need will be ours as a gift from God who "calls things that are not as though they were" (Rom. 4:17).

As a faith community we were specific about our

57

needs and concrete about our plans to occupy the "land" God wanted to give us. Denominational approval to purchase the building came along with a $15,000 check. Other Christian and secular groups caught the vision: The Christian Broadcast Network pledged $15,000. The Shubert Foundation, one of Broadway's most generous theater organizations, pledged $15,000. Combined with our own modest funds, the $47,500 deposit was made on the property. An aggressive campaign to raise the remaining capital began, and Christians across the country contributed to the dream.

As the appointed date for the close of escrow approached, tension mounted. It looked as though we would lose our option to buy the Lambs Club. We still lacked $57,000. Knowing that it was God who originally opened the door of opportunity and that the dream of owning property was a vision from above, we trusted God who began the good work to see it through completion.

D-Day arrived, and we were caught short. A fifteen-day extension was granted. Five hours before the final deadline imposed by the bank, the Nazarene denomination came through with the balance needed for the $114,500 down payment on the building.

Lightning flashed, thunder roared, the windows of heaven were opened—or so it seemed—as we took possession of the "land" God had promised. The final papers were signed, and the Lambs became the *Lamb's*—the new home of Manhattan Church of the Nazarene.

Today, the Lamb's Center operates a medical clinic, a broadway theater, and a feeding program, provides social services, and is host to other Christian organizations that lease space from it. (The full story has been told in *Shepherd of Times Square*.)[1]

What my experience at the Lamb's and the example of Abraham teaches me is that God raises up leaders with

58

specific dreams and visions who can trust him for results. The Letter to the Hebrews reminds us that faith or vision "is the assurance of things hoped for, the conviction of things not seen" (Heb. 11:1 RSV). Every church spire points heavenward to a level of vision not yet achieved. And in every person, I believe, a dream lays hidden awaiting fulfillment through faith and obedience to a call.

The Call to a New City

Toward the end of my time in New York, while still in seminary, I lifted up my eyes and envisioned a new dream and ministry in San Francisco. During the winter break, I visited the city and walked its streets. I found myself one morning out on a hill overlooking the Golden Gate Bridge. There I caught a glimpse of what God wanted to do through me.

The vision was vague at first: I saw the fog rolling into San Francisco Bay, the Golden Gate beautifully suspended across the skyline, the city buildings in the background floating on the clouds, and the bright morning sun rising on the horizon. I thought for a moment I was gazing on the City of God in heaven. Then I remembered that "Golden Gate" is also the name of the "Beautiful Gate" in Jerusalem through which it is said the Messiah will come to set up God's kingdom. Would it not be glorious, I thought, to establish a community and mission by the name of Golden Gate?

God seemed to be saying through that image that the city of San Francisco was precious in his sight. The sun rising over the city, trying to shine through the fog, spoke to me of God trying to dispel the clouds of iniquity that surround this city and to shine in every human heart. I wanted to be part of what God was doing in San Francisco. I wanted to be a visionary leader through whom God could accomplish his purpose.

During my final year of seminary, I was preoccupied with thoughts of San Francisco. As I prayed, specific and clear-cut ideas rushed into my mind, which I recorded in my journal. I came up with a list of goals and objectives for Golden Gate Community:

- a Christian presence downtown, where most of the people are who hurt and cry, live and die;
- a church to be born, a community to grow, and a mission to be established for the poor;
- compassionate ministries involved in feeding the hungry, sheltering the homeless, clothing the needy, and offering hospitality for the stranger;
- counseling services, including an outreach into the gay community;
- an employment agency for homeless individuals who have the will to work;
- a religious bookstore, thrift shop, or other business ventures that would support the ministry.

I even dreamed about the possibility of someday securing an old ferryboat to serve as a Christian community center. I imagined it being docked between the wharf and the bridge, lit up at night and turned into the "Ark of Golden Gate." It would feature "Noah's Place" for delicious non-alcoholic drinks, "Gopherwood Café" for short-order snacks, "Ark of the Covenant Bookstore," offering the finest in religious books and records, and "Theater in the Ark," producing professional theater to God's glory. On Sundays it could be an "Ark of Worship" for God's people.

My vision was ambitious but my goals clear-cut. I had an intense, burning desire to minister in San Francisco. Before returning to New York after my winter break from seminary, Paul Moore, who had been my mentor for many years, gave me a majestic photograph of the Golden Gate Bridge to hang on my wall. It served as a symbolic reminder of the vision I had to someday start a Christian community and urban ministry in San Francisco. In the following months God used that photograph and the vision it represented as a thumb in my back encouraging me to find a way to realize the dream.

My vision for San Francisco was far ahead of the immediate task—graduating from seminary and releasing that in which I was involved in New York. I had to slow down and not let my vision get the best of me. As I prayed for assurance, a verse from *The Living Bible* confirmed that my vision, though premature, was from the Lord: "But these things I plan won't happen right away. Slowly, steadily, surely, the time approaches when the vision will be fulfilled. If it seems slow, do not despair, for these things will surely come to pass" (Hab. 2:3 TLB).

Step Two: Build It Slowly

After discerning God's will, patience is required in realizing the vision for urban ministry. In the same way as it takes a season for a seed planted in the ground to grow into a flower, or nine months for a fetus conceived in the womb to be born as a child, it takes years for a dream or vision in the heart to become reality.

What happens in you is as important as what God does through you. Be content to wait on the Lord, allow God to do a redemptive work in you, and then to build your dream slowly and surely.

As an urban minister in San Francisco, I have drawn inspiration from the patron saint of my city—Francis of Assisi, the humble thirteenth-century monk from Italy who radically lived the gospel. Christians, mystics, humanitarians, revolutionaries, animal lovers, and the poor are all enamored of his simple spirit of compassion and truth.

As a young man, Francis had a particular distaste for lepers. While riding horseback one fine day, he encountered a leper standing beside the road. Initially repulsed, then feeling a strong surge of compassion, Francis dismounted and put some money into the man's hands. "More is required of you," said a still, small voice in Francis's heart. In a dramatic gesture he would later regard as a turning point in his life, Francis kissed the leper. From that time on he gave away everything he owned and began to see himself as having a special bond with the poor and disadvantaged.

Later, Francis went to pray at the ruined old church of San Damiano. In a vision he received instructions from the Lord: "Rebuild my church, for it is in ruins."

Franco Zeffirelli's film on Francis, *Brother Sun, Sister Moon*, includes a moving scene of Francis rebuilding the ruined church. Alone at first, laying stone upon stone, he is joined by others who share his vision. Together they sing a song of simplicity and patience that has caught on among Francis enthusiasts.

> If you want your dream to be,
> Take your time, go slowly.
> Do few things but do them well.
> Heartfelt work grows purely.
>
> Day by day, stone by stone,
> Build your secrets slowly.
> Day by day, you'll grow too,
> You'll know heaven's glory.
>
> If you want to live life free,
> Take your time, go slowly.
> Do few things but do them well,
> Heartfelt joys are holy.[2]

Reflecting back on my New York experience, the dream began purely enough. The community took time to *be* before *doing* a lot of ministry activities. However, the pace accelerated and the "tyranny of the urgent" rushed in. The result was crisis ministry: never-ending demands, overwhelming needs, too little money, ministries spread too thin, and staff burn-out. For years we struggled to survive until we slowed down and took the necessary time for reflective thinking, ministry focus, and spiritual grounding.

The intensity of urban ministry threatens to destroy even the most confident visionary. The way to "live life free" is to let your vision unfold slowly, "day by day, stone by stone," following the rhythm of the Spirit.

Step Three: Recruit Co-Workers

A visionary cannot fulfill God's dream alone. The vision must be shared by others. Finding the right people takes time. Recruit associates you know and trust, who are competent, committed, and whom you can confide in and enjoy. Don't bring people along simply because they are eager and available. Wait for called and gifted co-workers who will be companions on the journey.

It took me over a year to find five willing and able co-workers to join me in San Francisco in community. It took another seven years to establish Golden Gate Community as a church and mission. Jesus himself spent three years making disciples of twelve men and a group of women. Only then did he say to Peter, "feed my lambs" and, "on this rock I will build my church" (John 21:17; Matt. 16:18).

The first year of a new church or ministry is always the most exciting. A story is in the making that will be remembered and passed on in the organization's history. Everything is fun (at least in retrospect) and each event has significance. Try to record it all in story form. It will help you and your community remember and give thanks when times get difficult.

Step Four: Adopt a Neighborhood

After recruiting co-workers, the next step is to slowly and prayerfully identify a particular neighborhood in which to minister. Ask the hard questions: Who are the people God is calling us to love? What blocks or geographical areas seem most in need of Christ's presence? What neighborhoods seem ripe for urban ministry?

Every city has neglected quarters. Every town has a skid row, and everywhere there are people who live "on the other side of the tracks." We can have visions for reaching entire cities, but urban ministry is most effective when focused on a particular neighborhood.

There are always certain neighborhoods that are better suited than others to be urban mission fields. Choose an area that has a history, a profile, and a personality—one that attracts and challenges you. Most important, adopt a neighborhood where the poor are found!

Golden Gate Community felt a particular attraction to the Haight Ashbury district. As a teenager, I had visited the neighborhood in the sixties during the "Summer of Love." Inspired by a dream that life has more to offer than the Establishment's materialism, America's flower children arrived in droves in San Francisco. The signs of the times were everywhere: long hair, freaky clothes, love beads, waterpipes, drugs, sex, rock and roll.

I walked the same streets in the seventies when Haight Ashbury had become a haven for drug addicts.

The hippies had abandoned the buildings, and businesses were boarded up. The Haight of the eighties, with its high visibility and counterculture, beckoned as a great place to start a church and establish a mission. We intentionally chose this neighborhood in order to focus our ministry on the homeless population that has historically gravitated to the parks and alleyways off Haight Street.

Step Five: Secure an Outpost

Securing an outpost in the chosen neighborhood is the next essential step in starting an urban ministry. Ideally, lease or buy a building that has a cultural profile and easy access for the public. The people that you seek to reach need a symbol of your commitment and presence. Communities require living space, and ministries need room to grow. A neighborhood center fulfills these needs.

Within our first year, we purchased a large Victorian house in Haight Ashbury. Built in 1891, it survived the 1906 San Francisco earthquake and had become a landmark. Local residents remember it as a hippie commune in the sixties and one of the houses in which legendary rock star Janis Joplin lived. It had also been the home of a UFO cult whose leader claimed to be an archangel in touch with extraterrestrial activity and whose members believed in a new messiah who would descend in a flying saucer.

The Oak Street House, as we called it, was four stories tall with sixteen rooms, including two kitchens, two dining rooms, two living rooms, seven bedrooms, and three bathrooms. The facility seemed perfectly suited for a community house and mission center. The price tag in 1981—$290,000!

In fear and trembling, I signed a sixty-day contract to

assume the existing loan and make a $60,000 down payment. Clearly, our capital-poor community was out on a limb of faith. The five of us shared our dream every Sunday morning and evening and Wednesday nights in Nazarene churches across the district. We challenged 60 people to give $1,000, or 120 to give $500, to "buy a piece of the Oak."

After six weeks of aggressive fundraising, we had $20,000. One week before the down payment was due, we had $30,000, half of what was needed. In a state of panic, I called a critical meeting. We gained reassurance through prayer and voted to continue believing and looking to God as our source.

On a Sunday, with five precious days to go, I spoke to two local Nazarene churches about our need. Both took offerings and made pledges of over $7,000 each. We were up to $45,000! The day before the close of escrow, we lacked only $10,000. I thought of getting on the phone and asking everyone I knew for an emergency loan or an extension of funds from their credit cards. Instead, I called a prayer meeting, and we simply waited on the Lord.

An unexpected phone call came from my home church in Pasadena, California. "We want to pledge $5,000 for the ministry house, and we'll present it to you when you come down to speak next month," said the representative. "Thank you," I replied, "but escrow closes tomorrow! Can you wire it up today?" They did!

A second phone call came from a businessman in Eureka, California, with a personal pledge of $2,500. "I'm putting it in the mail today," he said. "Thank you, but can you wire it down today?" He did. That same day the balance needed came in the mail, over the wire, or in person for a total of $60,500!

With the cashier's check in hand, I paraded down to the escrow office to claim title to the ministry house that practical wisdom said could not be purchased in sixty days by a five-member community with no assets. Miracles are acts of God with precise timing. Trusting God for a miraculous start served to remind us when times got rough of God's eleventh-hour provisions. I know from personal experience, both in New York and San Francisco, that there is no such thing as an impossible dream.

Step Six: Build Community

The five of us who moved into the Oak Street House were anxious to establish a Christian presence in the neighborhood. Our immediate task, however, was getting our own house in order and learning to live with each other under one roof. The principle is this: Before mission involvement in your adopted neighborhood, your group must become a community.

What is community? J. B. Libanio, writing about Christian base communities in Central and South America, defines it this way: "A dynamic unit of persons that through spontaneous social interaction becomes integrated by bonds of friendship, emotional ties, common history and culture."[3]

A community is formed when a small group integrates, journeys together, and wants to do something greater than they individually could ever achieve. Gordon Cosby, pastor of the Church of the Savior in Washington, D.C., has spent the past forty years developing community through what he calls "mission groups." A mission group, he says, "is a small group of people (five to twelve) conscious of the action of the Holy Spirit in their lives, enabling them to hear the call of God through Christ, to belong in love to one another, and offer the gift of their concrete life for the world's healing and unity."[4]

67

As a community of five, we felt called to live among the people we wished to reach. This required a long-term commitment. We were convinced, owing to numerous failed attempts by other groups, that Haight Ashbury residents and the street population would not be reached for Christ through mass evangelism or door-to-door canvassing. But if a small core of committed Christians lived together in their neighborhood, loved each other as the body of Christ, and exemplified that love to others outside the community by providing a needed service, there was a chance of success.

Community means commitment to each other and to God's plan of reconciliation. Community is necessary before worship and mission can properly take place. A ministry group that hopes to reach a city, neighborhood, or block with the love of God must first love and honor its members.

Golden Gate Community nearly disbanded in its first year, learning the lessons of the common life. Differences in personality, theology, background, standards of work and cleanliness, gifts, and calling can either destroy a group or forge it into essential unity. We survived and prospered, but only through commitment to the process and focus on the vision.

Step Seven: Let Mission Flow

A small Christian community organized for the sake of mission and meeting at least once a week for worship, prayer, and support has the potential to discern what God is doing and to become part of it. Gordon Cosby's *Handbook for Mission Groups* describes step by step how such communities are formed and how they find their ministry.

Initially, a group gathers around a visionary (or a small nucleus of persons) who has heard a call for a

specific ministry and has sounded that call in a variety
of ways—in personal conversation, in leadership ability, or in prophetic witness. "The fire of God kindled
within his or her own spirit inflames others."[5]

If no one responds, the called person waits for the
moment others can share it. When two or three respond,
they begin their life together, "evoking one another's
gifts, and praying for clarity in hearing God's will as to
their mission."[6]

The call may begin with one person sensing the still,
small voice (image, feeling) of God saying "feed my
hungry," "shelter my homeless," or "comfort my
people with AIDS." As others respond to the call,
implications and ramifications are seen. An important
principle of mission groups is that mutual commitment
is needed and shared responsibility accepted by every
member. "This can be done only by discovering and
calling forth the gifts of each group member," says
Cosby. "If even one or two members have not identified
their gifts," he warns, "the problem of pride and envy
will surface."[7]

Multi-gifted persons will face the temptation of
wanting to experience the ego satisfaction of individual
effort rather than community spirit. Without commitment to a corporate life and mission, even if this means
long-term sacrifice and unfulfilled expectations, a
community will not outlast its leader.

With commitment to group process and perseverance, a mission community may last a season or a
lifetime. The work that is done will be the work of
Christ and be forever part of the activity of God's
reconciling efforts in the world.

Sometimes, a group fulfills its mission and comes to
an end. What should happen when a community dies a
natural death? According to Cosby, "When there are no
longer two or more called members in a group and this is
recognized, the group may review its history, give

thanks for the months or years of its life, and celebrate its death. Often there is an awareness of sin to be forgiven, grief to be healed, and courage needed for the next steps to be taken."[8]

If a mission group survives its formative stage and God clearly is directing, then ministries will be established. Enthusiasm will be seasoned with wisdom, innovation will be tempered by tradition, and a multitude of interested persons will be directed by God to support and assist the community's efforts. The mission community may remain part of an established church congregation or may develop separately as a provisional worshiping community and mission center.

In the case of Golden Gate Community, what began as a personal vision became a community of five and then eight. Soon there were a dozen of us. Some of the original members left and others came to continue the dream. A neighborhood was adopted, an outpost secured, and a mission established. Compassionate ministries, including feeding the hungry, sheltering the homeless, clothing the needy, training the unemployed, and assisting persons with AIDS were developed in due course. Golden Gate Ministries was formed as the umbrella organization for these neighborhood ministries.

Golden Gate Ministries gave birth to a local church that grew and relocated to larger facilities. Golden Gate Community Church of the Nazarene found ways to return to its roots to support the mission from whence it came. With mutuality and support, the church became a faith community of the mission, and the mission became a ministry expression of the church.

Notes

1. Paul Moore, *Shepherd of Times Square* (Nashville: Thomas Nelson Books, 1978).
2. Donovan Leitch, "Little Church." Copyright 1973 and 1974 by Famous Music Corporation.
3. J. B. Libanio, "Understanding Christian Base Communities," *Transformation* 3, no. 3 (July/September 1986).
4. Gordon Cosby, *Handbook for Mission Groups* (Washington, D.C.: Church of the Savior, n.d.), p. 2.
5. Ibid.
6. Ibid., p. 7.
7. Ibid., pp. 8-9.
8. Ibid., p. 12.

4

TAKING IT TO THE STREETS
Community Action and Development

The only gospel most people will ever read is the gospel written on your life. —Francis of Assisi

Basically, there are two brands of urban ministries—specialized ministries and community-based ministries. Specialized ministries are those with a selected "target group" and a strategy for helping or reaching that particular group for Christ. (Chuck Colson's Prison Fellowship, for instance, is an example of a specialized ministry targeting prisons that need reform and prisoners who need the Lord.) A community-based ministry, on the other hand, targets a particular neighborhood and seeks to assess and address the needs of that chosen community the best it can. Both specialized and community-based ministries are valid and needed; however, this chapter is about how to become active in your neighborhood and develop a community-based ministry.

In my study, which overlooks Haight Street, a translation of a poem written in China by Dr. Y. C. James Yen is posted on my bulletin board. In starting a community-based ministry, I have meditated often on these words:

Go to the people.
Live among them.
Learn from them.
Plan with them.
Work with them.
Start with what they know.
Build on what they have.
Teach by showing; learn by doing.
Not a showcase, but a pattern.
Not odds and ends, but a system
Not piecemeal, but integrated approach.
Not to conform, but to transform.
Not relief but release.[1]

Dr. Yen's "Credo of Rural Reconstruction" was developed after working with Chinese peasant people in the 1920s and has been applied by his organization to rural reconstruction in many Third World countries. It equally can be applied to urban development. In order to do this, our Western thinking about evangelism must change.

Zealous groups of Christians come and go in the city. Typically, expensive auditoriums are rented for evangelistic crusades, outdoor rallies and concerts are held in city parks and on the streets, Bibles are distributed door to door, "surveys" are conducted, and tracts are handed out to busy people passing by.

Sometimes these tactics result in friendly encounters and saved lives. More often, the crusade ends, the concert is over, the street ministry team goes home, and the city returns to normal. Local groups try to follow up on "prime contacts" made at the rallies, but by that time the contact is cold and the mood is different. While an inner-city evangelistic blitz raises consciousness (and eyebrows), it offers little for city people's felt needs and seldom has long-lasting effects.

Although I have participated in many such special events over the years, I am convinced that there is a better way. To plant and grow an urban church or mission, the ministering body must be community-based. Denominational agendas must be relinquished, and leadership must work behind the scene. What we understand as "church" must not be hidden behind stained-glass walls but taken to the streets.

To know and love the poor, we must journey with them. To journey with the poor means to go and live among them; to seek to understand their needs, hopes, and dreams; to walk a few miles in their shoes; to learn from them and suffer with them; to build bridges; to channel resources; to do what can be done.

To journey with the poor means to open up your home, to be hospitable, to break bread together, to find common ground.

To journey with the poor means to be of service; to equip and empower people; to work side by side; to plan, build, and teach.

Above all, when all is said and done, it means to refuse the spotlight and to let the people say, "We have done it ourselves."

Once an urban mission has been planted, there are a half dozen steps in building community-based ministries that are effective and long lasting: (1) *build neighborhood awareness*; (2) *assess its needs*; (3) *network with others*; (4) *gain a profile for service*; (5) *empower people to be released*; (6) *lead so that others get the credit*.

Community Awareness

Every neighborhood has a history and a personality. In some cities, every block is an ethnic village. Whoever the people are that God has called you to, wherever they live, go and live among them. Try to understand their turf. Begin by defining the boundaries of the area you want to reach, both geographically and by the type of people found there. Then, identify significant features of your neighborhood. What schools and hospitals are nearby? Where are the police and fire stations located? Where do people hang out? What are the hot spots for local encounters and activities? Which businesses are well accepted, and which ones do people resent? What cafés and restaurants do people like, and why? What newspapers do people read, and why do they read them?

During the first six months of starting an urban mission in San Francisco, I walked up Haight Street to the park nearly every day. I stood on that famous corner of Haight and Ashbury and tried to sense the changes since the sixties. I usually had coffee at the Grand Piano, a casual coffeehouse popular with the locals. In a pleasant atmosphere of classical music, with newspapers and pamphlets spread all over and where breakfast was served all day, it was easy to strike up conversations and find out about the Haight.

An important part of community awareness is to recognize and call neighborhood folks by their names. In time they will come to accept you as part of the turf. I remember being initially amazed at how many "old timers" from the sixties were known by their assumed names: Uncle Huck, Blue Jay Way, Tree, Rainbow, Ranger, Mojo, Indian Sue, Cosmic Lady, Tri-Lite, Stealer, Dirtman.

Awareness means to be genuinely interested in all sorts of people. Seek solidarity with them. Try to find out people's interests and the values that motivate their actions. It helps to keep a notebook and record your contacts and what they tell you about themselves and the community. Write down data, insights, and resource information for future reference.

Think in terms of "my people," "my land," "this is where I pitch my tent"—not possessively but responsibly, with solidarity and compassion. Don't be detached. Instead, make people's welfare your concern, remembering the words of the prophet: "Seek the welfare of the city where I have sent you into exile, and pray to the

75

LORD on its behalf, for in its welfare you will find your welfare" (Jer. 29:7-8 RSV).

Community awareness also means that sooner or later, you personally will need to move into the neighborhood you have prayed for, identified with, and desire to reach. This can be a difficult and sacrificial step of faith, as my wife and I remember.

I began ministry in San Francisco by living in our community house in the neighborhood. Single at the time and more simple in lifestyle, one room in a household of seven was enough. When I married Rebecca Laird three years later, we opted for more space in a safer neighborhood in church-owned property across the Bay in Berkeley.

That decision was a great way to start a marriage, and we enjoyed a comfortable year of homemaking and retreat from the city. But after fifteen months of commuting an hour and a half to the mission field, we were compelled to move back to San Francisco.

We both had read a decisive article entitled "Comfort, Community and Missions" by Moishe Rosen, director of Jews for Jesus, which convinced us that the time to move was now. In the article Rosen asserts:

- An urban evangelist must live in the community to be reached.
- An urban evangelist must associate with the people he or she hopes to reach and win to Christ.
- An urban evangelist must learn to understand the thinking of those to be reached.[2]

Rosen recalled an earlier time when he lived in the suburbs and commuted thirty-two miles daily to minister in the city. "I spent three precious hours every day travelling instead of ministering. Not only that, but living so far from those I wanted to reach discouraged me from building the kind of relationships I should have had in order to be most effective."[3]

After considerable struggle, we left our comfortable Berkeley Hills home and embraced the city again. We rented a nice apartment, recently renovated after being a squat for the homeless for many years, on the busy corner of Haight and Masonic streets, just four blocks from the mission center. I remember our first night back in the city, and Rebecca's reflection on the decision we had made.

The street sounds and rumbling of five bus lines have replaced the serenity of the hills. When we look out of our new turret window, we no longer see the deer that came to chew on the fruit trees in our backyard in Berkeley. Instead we see Uganda Liquors, Reckless Records, and the Aquarian Foundation, one of the neighborhood's "New Age" churches. The Holey Bagel deli and a check-cashing service border the front door to our blue Victorian building, built in 1882. I awoke to the sounds of a street musician strumming "House of the Rising Sun" on his electric guitar in the doorway downstairs. Before we were ready to face the day, reality sunk in—we were back in the city, living among the people we are called to reach.

We soon were acclimated to city life again, and happy in our new home. Whatever sacrifice was initially required was replaced with greater blessing. Home is where the heart can be at rest, and if you are called to the city, your heart will find its rest on city streets with city people, beholding the beauty of the human landscape and journeying with those God has entrusted to your care.

Community awareness begins with the questions, To

what neighborhood and among what persons am I called to serve? Community awareness does not end until you have gone and lived among them, until their needs become associated with your own needs, until you sense solidarity with those to whom you minister.

Need Assessment

To reach people and win them to Christ, you must come to know their needs—not just the needs you think they have but the needs they really feel. Whether you adopt a block or a neighborhood, much listening and learning must take place before you can build on what the people already have. That is why a careful assessment of needs is essential.

When I arrived in Haight Ashbury in 1981, fourteen thousand residents lived within fifty square blocks. Demographically, blacks, representing 44 percent of the population, were moving out and whites, representing 39 percent, were moving in. Although San Francisco was 22 percent Asian and 17 percent Hispanic, few lived in the Haight. The gay community comprised at least a third of the neighborhood population in all age groups. Twenty-one percent of the population were under eighteen years of age; 43 percent were married adults; and 14 percent were seniors.

Although the living standards in the Haight were climbing, street people still dominated the human landscape. By choice or circumstance, they lived in the parks, in buses and vans along the panhandle, or in abandoned buildings called "squats."

Besides the usual street population of alcoholics, drug addicts, domestic pilgrims, and displaced immigrants, there was a new group to deal with—"skinheads" espousing anarchy and neo-nazism, who referred to the peace-loving hippies as "old-timers" and were often hostile and violent in their attitudes and actions. The

Haight of the late seventies and early eighties was a neighborhood in transition with an international profile and an ever-changing counterculture.

Other church groups had told us what they thought were the major problems of the neighborhood: burned-out hippies, homosexual infiltration, drug and alcohol abuse, high crime, and left-wing politics. When we asked local residents and street folks what were their needs, we got a different set of answers: affordable housing, jobs, access to health care and social services, and places to go during the day where they would be welcome.

Local groups and agencies are good sources of community information. Simple surveys and interviews can be conducted to compare and confirm the findings of others. Informal conversations on the street can provide useful data.

Technically, "need identification" refers to health and social service requirements in a community, whereas "need assessment" is aimed at determining the relative importance of these needs for the purpose of program planning. Both disciplines are necessary if appropriate community action is to take place. Both should be done systematically:·

1. Utilize existing information resources from national, regional, state and city depositories.[4]

2. Contact existing neighborhood agencies already addressing needs to obtain the information they possess.

3. Survey a cross section of the population who are potential "clients."

4. Walk the streets with your antennae out, observing needs firsthand and developing new information.

5. Hold a community forum where citizens can express their opinions about community needs.

6. Conduct informational interviews with key merchants, consumers, service providers, political leaders, educators, police, clergy, and local personalities with firsthand knowledge of the community's needs.

7. Integrate all relevant information gathered and assess its importance for program planning.

As apparent needs are identified, assessed, and addressed, deeper spiritual and psychological needs, less obvious to most persons, can be uncovered through Christian love and nurture. However, one must earn the right to point out spiritual and psychological needs by first helping persons with the apparent needs they immediately feel. We must feed the hungry, clothe the naked, shelter the homeless, and intervene in crisis, in the name of Christ. Then we may at the right time and in the right way explain to those who are interested God's plan of salvation.

Alex was an unwanted child when his mother bore him out of wedlock. He was six weeks old when he was adopted by a middle-class family in Ohio. At fifteen, Alex rebelled and ran away from home. He hitchhiked across the country, surviving on the streets the best he could. For ten years he stayed in shelters, ate in soup kitchens, crashed with friends, and hustled money on the streets by selling himself to men. Drugs, alcohol, and sexual favors became his life.

Alex wandered into the Oak Street House one summer for food, shelter, and clothing. After his basic needs were met, he was invited to attend a Friday night hospitality activity at the house. A Christian film was being shown and its message reached Alex's heart.

The next day Alex was helping to sort clothes in the clothing room with Peter, a staff volunteer. The more they shared what the ministry was all about, the more Alex wanted what he saw in Peter. He prayed to receive Christ into his life in the clothing room. The next week he moved into a room in the house and committed himself to a program design for men in transition from street survival to responsible Christian life. Alex's story is a reminder that street folks find the Lord in the context of their "felt needs" being known and met.

Through a need assessment, Golden Gate Community determined that part of our mission in the Haight was to help the homeless cope with life on the streets. We discovered in our study that San Francisco had a homeless population of eight to ten thousand and that a tenth of them were in our neighborhood. We offered what resources we had—an open house, hospitality, spiritual direction, and Christian community.

Before designing our own social service programs to address the needs of the homeless, we chose to contact existing agencies that had already become places of help and hope in the neighborhood. This essential step is called networking.

Building a Network

City people have overwhelming needs. No single church, mission, or agency can do it all. Networking is required, ecumenically, institutionally, and politically. Networking simply means being connected and knowing how to get a person the help required. There is no need to duplicate services. Instead, find places of help and hope and build on what is already there.

It may appear that a particular neighborhood is totally neglected and forsaken, devoid of Christian or even humanitarian presence. But this is seldom the case. If you are aware of your community, you will discover the presence of storefront churches, fellowship groups, community-action organizations, social service agencies, urban institutions, community-based programs, and other signs of hope. By identifying needs and existing services, a new community group can network with others to extend the resources.

Ecumenical Networking

Find out how many churches are located in your neighborhood, and determine their reputation for community involvement. Some will be invisible churches ("never heard of First Church") while others will enjoy a solid reputation for service ("Oh yeah, I go there for meals"). Build bridges to those churches that are active in the community. Share ideas, information, resources, equipment, volunteers, and property. Hold joint services on special occasions. Appear at each other's events. Sit on each other's program boards. Sow seeds of goodwill in the spirit of unity and friendship. Under the pressure of crisis or special need, network churches will band together and cooperate on a common cause.

When we moved into the Haight, there were at least twenty churches (counting all the storefronts and house churches), but only four with significant neighborhood profiles. All Saints Episcopal Church ran a Saturday morning feeding program and wanted to start an emergency shelter. Hamilton United Methodist

Church was hosting Alcoholics Anonymous meetings and was willing to host a soup kitchen and a family shelter, if there was community support. Mount Zion Baptist Church engaged in political action from time to time, but was less involved in the immediate neighborhood. Saint Agnes, a Roman Catholic church, was large and seemed content to offer mass and make referrals. The "New Age" Holistic Center and the occult-oriented Aquarian Foundation on Haight Street had their own followings and agendas but were not considered by many to be places of help and hope.

Our little Nazarene house-church wanted to join the ranks of the four established churches, so we made ourselves available for cooperative ministry. After a year or two of extended hospitality, referring contacts, and gaining the community's goodwill and acceptance, three churches came together and agreed to sponsor a triad of tangible services. A daily meal would be offered at Hamilton, overnight shelter would be offered at All Saints, and Golden Gate Community Church of Nazarene would offer clothes, hygiene kits, and evening snacks, issue bed vouchers for the shelter, and channel funds and volunteers.

Over the years, each of these ministries took on a life and identity of its own. The Haight Ashbury Soup Kitchen became a community collective feeding 250 people a day. The Haight Ashbury Family Shelter grew out of the need to house up to twenty families eating in the soup kitchen. The All Saints Shelter continued taking in forty to fifty men each night during the rainy season in the city. Golden Gate Community, responding to over five hundred mission clients, added to their hospitality ministry three other programs: social services, residency, and job development. In time, we became the hub of the network wheel.

The three church groups did together what none of them could have done separately—feed, clothe, shelter, and employ the poor and homeless, in Jesus' name. Each church was not primarily concerned with taking credit for the programs they were sponsoring. Rather, they were content to build the kingdom together with the means at their disposal. Clearly, there is no limit to the good that can be done when it matters not who gets the credit!

Networking is not only the key to compassionate ministry in the city, it is the essential link to resources outside the city limits. It has been said that 70 percent of the people live in the city, where only 30 percent of the resources are to be found, while 30 percent of the people live outside the city, where 70 percent of the resources are to be found.[5]

This being the case, inner-city churches and missions must be adopted by suburban congregations in order to connect resources with needs. Urban ministries can only survive if they are supported by those on the outside who know the needs and want to help. Golden Gate Community, for example, would not be able to survive if Nazarene churches across the country did not sponsor its ministries financially and with goodwill.

Institutional Networking

It is important to build bridges to other service organizations and agencies, both Christian and secular. Your clients need what others offer because you cannot do everything yourself. In urban ministry, churches and organizations must join hands and hang together to address crises and needs.

Enter into creative partnerships with others: "You screen, we'll service," or, "You host, we'll deliver." Refuse competition and risk cooperative ministry. Give and take ownership. Exchange favors. Offer financial resources or staffing for joint ownership and sponsorship. Think in terms of making deposits and withdrawals from the community service network bank.

Every member of your staff or mission group should join and become effectively involved in another community organization. Visibility and presence for your urban mission is directly proportional to your individual visibility and presence in the community network. By assisting other groups and organizations, your ministry will benefit in the process. It's a spiritual principle: "Give, and it will be given to you. A good measure, pressed down, shaken together and running over, will be poured into your lap. For with the measure you use, it will be measured to you" (Luke 6:38).

In Haight Ashbury, there were a dozen organizations to join or volunteer for. Golden Gate Community divided up the pie, with individual members joining the boards of the Haight Ashbury Soup Kitchen and Family Shelter, the Mayor's Task Force for the Homeless, and the neighborhood block association, S.A.F.E. Others volunteered for ministry at the Haight Ashbury Children's Center, the Earl Paltangi Youth Center, the Haight Ashbury Free Medical Clinic, the Haight Ashbury Switchboard, and the Community Hospice Center.

In a world where actions speak louder than words, infiltrating the neighborhood through community action and networking serves to establish your presence and allows the church to be heard.

Political Networking

Build bridges to city government, corporations, institutions, and local merchants without compromising ministry integrity. Although some associations make strange bedfellows, you need to know whom you can call on for resources.

After six years of building bridges in my neighborhood, the president of the Haight Ashbury Merchants'

Association called me to say, "The merchants have a project we want you to assist us with. We've established a fund to employ some of the homeless to clean up the streets. Can you screen and send us some of your clients?" We sent her a crew and organized an ongoing effort that became known as the Haight Ashbury Works Program. It gained national attention as an effective way to employ the homeless and restore dignity to some needy people. The opportunity flowed naturally out of years of political networking.

In any community there are key players and power-brokers who use their clout to control the game. Urban missionaries who heed Christ's call to be wise as serpents and harmless as doves will make it their business to know what motivates these principal players, how to push their hot buttons, and how to make their self-interest work for you. Their power, influence, and resources need to be redeemed and brought into your ministry network.

As a place to start, I recommend that priority be given to contacts with community leaders whose support you cannot afford to be without. Make appointments to see the following people, so that you can call on them should you need their help:

- Police captain of your neighborhood precinct
- Newspaper journalists and television reporters assigned to your area
- Bank presidents and branch managers
- Local politicians sensitive to community needs
- School principals and superintendents
- A member of the Planning Commission
- A representative of the mayor's office
- An official in city government

Through political networking, Golden Gate Community was able to gain access to housing through the mayor's office, cooperation from the police department, free consultation from corporate contacts, and program sponsorship through contacts at the University of San Francisco.

The goodwill generated and the networking that can evolve from key contacts will prove invaluable as your ministry unfolds. But ecumenical, institutional, and political networking are only possible if your ministry gains a reputation for service.

Gaining a Profile

More than a decade in the city has convinced me of the truth of the words of Saint Francis: "The only gospel most people will ever read is the gospel written on your life." Words alone do not communicate the gospel of our Lord. Actions speak louder than words, compassion backs up what we say, and unconditional love and acceptance provide the church access to streets.

As Christians we are called not to debate the words of Jesus but to do the works of Jesus. "You will do greater works than I," Jesus told his disciples—greater not in quality but in quantity. Urban Christians, as part of the continuing incarnation of Christ in the world, should dedicate themselves to doing the works of Jesus on the streets of the city.

The church or urban ministry committed to this purpose will be visible in the community and have a reputation for service. Without a ministry profile, it is doomed to failure or lost in insignificance.

Why is old First Church invisible to the community while Pilgrim's Rest Ebenezer Baptist Church is well known and respected? Because old First Church, somewhere along the way, stopped serving its community, became a commuter church, and lost touch with the neighborhood. Pilgrim's Rest, on the other hand, stayed involved in the community and was available to serve, and this is reflected even in its name.

Community involvement is important anywhere, but especially in the city where the very survival of a church or an urban mission depends on its reputation in the community.

Shortly after Golden Gate Community began ministry in the Haight, a Pentecostal group with lots of zeal moved into the neighborhood. The sponsoring mother-church in Los Angeles intended to duplicate itself in San Francisco and redeem our particular neighborhood. The local branch closed within the year. Why? Because it alienated residents and neighborhood organizations by its professed mission agenda, which was perceived as being anti-gay and insensitive to community needs. It failed to gain a reputation for community service. A combination of political pressure and personal discouragement caused the group to give up, shake the dust off its feet, and go elsewhere.

Golden Gate Community had moved into the same suspicious and potentially hostile neighborhood, yet overcame possible defeat. We, too, were viewed initially as "Bible thumpers" and "Moral Majority types" out to save the world. Complaints were registered that we discriminated against gays, and that we were holding public services in a residential area without a conditional use permit. City Planning cited us for building code violations that were not applied to others. We were told that only two families could live in the Oak Street House, not a community of seven who took in the homeless. Our clothing rooms were said to be unsafe, sprinklers were required on the first floor ceilings, and the brick stairway to the front door would have to be removed.

Total compliance with city requirements would have cost of thousands of dollars we didn't have. A conditional-use permit would be a year in process with no guarantee of being granted. I had just read of a Buddhist house church in the city being denied the use permit they applied for. These and other obstacles had to be overcome, the key to which was the goodwill of the neighborhood.

As pastor, I decided to call upon our neighborhood network for help and support in time of need. Fortunately, we had gained a reputation of being of service in our community. I credit the Lord and the goodwill of the people for the fact that the city dropped its complaints against us.

A reputation for service and a profile of ministry is like a city on a hill that cannot be hidden. It has light for all the world to see and rejoice in. This is what Jesus meant when he said, "Let your light shine before men, that they may see your good deeds and praise your Father in heaven" (Matt. 5:16).

How does a church or mission group raise its profile, remain visible, and shine with good deeds that inspire praise for God? Simply be involved in people's lives, be available for service, and affect change through compassionate ministry in Jesus' name.

Empower People

A bearer of God's light neither hides it under a bush nor imposes it on others. Rather, one simply shines it on people, one at a time, by word and deed, and then steps back to see if a new light has been lit.

It is important to meet people at the point of their need and gently lead them toward the light. This calls for patience and empowerment, with a friendly reminder that God is always at our elbows with strength and help for the impossible task.

Empowerment is the ability to give persons the resources and encouragement they need to believe the truth—"I can do everything through [Christ] who gives me strength" (Phil. 4:13).

It helps me to think of urban ministry as having two hands: One hand reaches out in compassion to relieve people's pain; the other takes people by the hand and stays by their side until they find release from that which causes the pain. Relief work—a cup of cold water, a hot meal, warm clothes, a blanket for the night—demonstrates God's love in a tangible way. Release work—healing and deliverance, spiritual victory, resolution of personal issues, learning life skills for success and work skills for gainful employment—makes disciples of people in every area of their lives.

The old Chinese proverb bears repeating: "If you give a man a fish, he can eat for a day. If you teach a man to fish, he can eat for a lifetime."

Empowering people for a lifetime of successful Christian living requires that we take the time necessary to invest in their futures. Show the hungry how to utilize resources effectively. Teach the sick preventive medicine. Help the homeless get back on their feet. Equip the unemployed with tools and work skills. Facilitate the psychologically traumatized in working out their issues. Structure community life to impart principles for managing time, talents, finances, and relationships. Above all, point the way for those who hunger and thirst after righteousness to be filled with God's blessings. This is the real challenge of urban ministry.

Indirect Leadership Is Key

Servant leadership is essential for community action and development, as in any ministry. Without clear directions, people are like sheep without a shepherd, and do not know where to turn. Strong, visionary, consistent, tenacious, innovative servant leadership is required.

God always raises up someone to sound the call, inspire others to gather around, and skillfully steer the ship of ministry through both safe and troubled waters. Communities that have no leader or too many leaders generally do not last. A community, church, or mission is only as strong as the persons in charge.

The best leaders have an invisible presence. They work behind the scenes. Without asserting their authority too often, they keep a watchful eye on what is happening and are ready to nudge things to the left or right if necessary. You can recognize such a leader if he or she can accomplish goals through others without taking credit; if he or she can share power and responsibility; if he or she seeks not the limelight but is content with a job well done.

A leader's life is short-lived compared to that of the organization. If a leader wants what was begun to outlive himself or herself as founder, his or her leadership style must be participatory. What the apostle Paul cites as the role of pastors is equally true for all leaders: "to prepare God's people for works of service" (Eph. 4:12).

After the people are prepared, the best thing to do is to get out of the way and let ministry happen. A worthy goal is for leaders to work themselves out of their jobs and let new leaders take their places.

I found myself doing this periodically in my fifteen years of urban ministry. As associate pastor of the Lamb's mission in New York, I let go after five years and started something new in San Francisco. After five years of planting and pastoring Golden Gate Community Church, I released it to more capable and sustaining hands and focused my efforts on directing the mission. After three years of developing the Oak Street House mission, I recruited and trained a mission director to run the programs. As pastor and director of Golden Gate Ministries, I know myself to be an urban missionary

91

gifted in the areas of development and implementation and in preparing others for service. I want to be the kind of leader who does not seek the limelight, but who gets out of the way when his work is done, so that the people can say, "We have done it ourselves."

The measure of success in urban ministry is that it is owned by the people. If they point to the leader and say, "He did it," the work is not indigenous and will not last. But if the people in need of help are also equipped and empowered, the work truly will be theirs and continue after the leader is gone.

Love says go to the people, live among them, work with them, take it to the streets. Journey with them and understand their needs. Become aware. Network with others. Build on what they have. Teach by example what is helpful. Do not be too proud to learn. Resist imposing programs and seek only to be of service. Do not leave behind a showcase but a pattern that others may follow. Do some relief work, yet do not be content until there is release. And when your task is accomplished and your work is done, let the people all remark, "We have done it ourselves!"

Notes

1. "Credo of Rural Reconstruction," Dr. James C. Yen, International Institute of Rural Reconstruction, Silang, Cavite, the Philippines. United States office: 1775 Broadway, New York, NY 10019. Used by permission.
2. Moishe Rosen, "Comfort, Community and Missions," *Jews for Jesus Newsletter* 7 (1986).
3. Ibid.
4. The following are sources of demographic information: Census Access for Planning in the Church, Concordia

Teachers College, River Forest, IL 60305; National Decision Systems, 539 Encinitas Blvd., Encinitas, CA 92024; Population Reference Bureau, 1337 Connecticut Ave., N.W., Washington, D.C. 20036.
5. Paul Moore, "Master Plan: Here's Life Inner-City," unpublished paper written for Campus Crusade for Christ.

5

PRACTICING HOSPITALITY IN THE CITY
Making the Stranger into a Friend

Let every guest be received as Christ. —Saint Benedict

Hospitality means making a guest feel at home. By tracing the ministry of hospitality from its ancient roots, identifying two strands of biblical teaching on the subject, and telling stories, I hope to weave a tapestry depicting the church as a house of hospitality and refuge, and guests as gifts from God.

The way we use our homes and churches is an indication of our commitment to the ministry of hospitality. For some, their home is their castle or retreat from life's storms and troubles. They spend so much time with others at work or church that they need an off-limits residence to recover in. Others see their homes as hostels, open to whatever stranger passes by; people are coming and going all the time. Both extremes can be hindrances to true hospitality—the first due to the absence of guests, the second due to hospitality burn-out.

For some congregations, the church building is so sacred it is used only for worship and fellowship with Christians, never for the secular use of outside guests.

Other congregations see their mission as being perpetually open for prayer and services for whoever comes to the door. Again, both extremes can hinder the practice of biblical hospitality.

Hospitality in biblical times was practiced in response to the safety needs of travelers. At a time when motels and inns were nonexistent, those who sojourned were dependent on the goodwill and hospitality of hosts who would take them in, refresh them with a meal, and find them a place of shelter and safety for the night. Hostels, hotels, and hospitals grew out of the ancient practice, and the hospice movement today finds its roots in offering hospitality to the stranger on the way home.

Today, in the city, hospitality presents a different challenge. Risk and fear are major concerns. Not every stranger is to be trusted. Discernment is required and "testing the waters" is appropriate before opening up one's home or church to just anyone. Our fear of strangers goes back to our earliest warnings: Don't talk to strangers! Don't accept a ride from someone you do not know! Our fears my be well founded and the risks real, but the biblical injunction is to "offer hospitality to one another without grumbling" (I Peter 4:9).

The English word "hospitality" does not convey the original meaning of the Greek word *philoxenos*, which means "lover of strangers," in contrast to *philadelphia*, which means "kinship love." Biblical hospitality is an attitude of the heart that prepares for guests, welcomes pilgrims on long journeys, makes the stranger feel at home, and offers refuge to the sojourner. Father Henri Nouwen defines hospitality as "creating free and friendly space for guests" so that they feel honored and refreshed in your presence.[1]

Among those committed today to the ministry of hospitality, monks tend to be the most exemplary. Perhaps by seeing how those in the monastic tradition practice hospitality, we can better understand its place in the city, where the risks are greater, the costs higher, and the complications more challenging.

Monastic Hospitality

In the tiny village of Taizé, France, is an international community of fifty monks who receive an unbelievable number of visitors each year from all over the world. Pilgrims with tents and sleeping bags come from seven continents to experience the meditative worship and ecumenical dialogue that has made this monastery famous. Simple meals are served, basic accommodations provided, and as many as two thousand guests a week are made to feel at home.

I will never forget the hospitality extended to me as a stranger during my visit to Taizé. It was winter, and it took a day of complicated arrangements to travel from Paris to Taizé. A fast train, a bus connection, a taxi ride, and a final hike later, the bells of the monastery were in sight at the top of the winding village road. At the entrance was a yellow house of welcome with a roaring fireplace and registration desk. The suggested overnight donation was on a sliding scale depending on one's own needs and the standard of living of the country one was from.

Being married and over thirty, my wife and I were welcome to stay in the guest house rather than in the dormitory for the younger single crowd. Two small and simple beds in a private room with a shared bath down the hall were enough for weary pilgrims anxious for a night's rest.

Prayers of Taizé were chanted three times a day beginning at 8 A.M. in the Church of the Resurrection. The chapel was dark, majestic and candlelit, and able to expand to hold up to five thousand worshipers at one time. Following the evening service one night, Brother

Roger, founder and prior of Taizé, invited me and seven other guests to join him and seven brothers for a "meal" at their community house. We felt special as we were led almost ritualistically to a large, warm, candlelit room with another wonderful welcoming fireplace stoked with wood.

As meditative music played softly in the background, hot cocoa and cookies were served in silence to the guests. A warm cup had never felt so good, nor had cocoa ever tasted so delicious, as it had on that cold winter night in the company of Brother Roger. We prayed together and discussed the content of his annual Letter from Taizé, which would be translated into thirty languages and find its way to over one hundred thousand subscribers. Challenged, inspired, and refreshed, we were dismissed with a blessing.

Brother Roger and his community, in practicing the gentle art of simple hospitality, were witnessing to the biblical mandate of Jesus, who said, "I was a stranger and you invited me in" (Matt. 25:35). As a stranger, I was made to feel welcome. Though it was a simple meal served, careful preparations were made for entertaining guests. I felt important, and that my participation in the writing of the letter was valued. The experience has become my reference point in practicing hospitality in the city.

"Let every guest be received as Christ" has been the monastic rule since the fifth century, when Benedict wrote his rule for monks (Rule of Saint Benedict). Communities like Taizé and monasteries around the world have embraced hospitality as one of their spiritual disciplines. Monks tell an ancient story that illumines their practice of attending to the needs of strangers.

The Monk and the Cripple

Going to town one day to sell some small articles, Abba Agathon met a cripple on the roadside, paralyzed

97

in his legs, who asked him where he was going. Abba Agathon replied, "To town to sell some things." The other said, "Do me the favor of carrying me there." So he carried him to the town. The cripple said to him, "Put me down where you sell your wares." He did so. When he had sold an article, the cripple asked, "What did you sell it for?" and he told him the price. The other said, "Buy me a cake," and he bought it. When Abba Agathon had sold a second article, the sick man asked, "How much did you sell it for?" And he told him the price of it. Then the other said, "Buy me this," and he bought it. When Agathon, having sold all his wares, wanted to go, he said to him, "Are you going back?" and he replied, "Yes." Then he said, "Do me the favor of carrying me back to the place where you found me." Once more picking him up, he carried him back to that place. Then the cripple said, "Agathon, you are filled with divine blessings, in heaven and on earth." Raising his eyes, Agathon saw no man; it was an angel of the Lord, come to try him.[2]

Two Strands of Biblical Teaching

Biblically, when you receive another human being with a warmhearted welcome and loving-kindness, even if to render such service is inconvenient or unappreciated, you may be closer than you realize to a divine encounter. Welcoming the domestic stranger and offering refuge to the foreign sojourner are two major strands of biblical teaching. In weaving them together, we come to realize the ministry of hospitality.

Welcoming the Stranger

Abraham and Sarah were relaxing in the shade of their oak trees in Hebron when they were surprised by the appearance of three visitors. As gracious hosts, they welcomed the strangers, washed their feet, poured them a drink, and prepared them a meal. They turned out to be angels with a message from the Lord (Gen. 18).

Likewise, Lot entertained two men who visited him in Sodom. The sins of Sodom were pride, extravagance, immorality, and inhospitality to the poor and needy (Ezek. 16). Lot was saved because of his gracious spirit and concern for justice, while his city was destroyed by the visiting angels (Gen. 19).

The Letter to the Hebrews reminds us that we should show hospitality to strangers, for in so doing some have entertained angels, unaware that they were God's messengers (Heb. 13:1-6).

Jesus sent his disciples with instructions, but without provisions, to preach the gospel to the lost sheep of Israel. They were to seek and accept hospitality from worthy persons in the towns and villages they visited. "If anyone will not welcome you or listen to your words," they were told, "shake the dust off your feet when you leave that home or town." Those who failed to show hospitality to the disciples were rejecting Christ who sent them, while those who at least offered them a "cup of cold water" would not lose their reward (Matt. 10:14, 42).

Christ's teaching took a more mystical turn when he said, "as you did it to one of the least of these my brethren, you did it to me" (Matt. 25:40 RSV). We are left with the mysterious notion that every time we encounter a stranger in need, we are to look through that person and see Jesus. When we welcome "one of the least of these," we are welcoming Jesus. And when we fail to show hospitality and kindness to that person in our path, we are rejecting Jesus in the distressing disguise of the poor and needy stranger.

The Story of Elijah

Many strangers and street pilgrims find their way to Golden Gate Community's Oak Street House, but I've never met anyone like the bare-chested, barefoot, black stranger in a denim loincloth, with wild, matted hair down to his lower back, who showed up one night in the winter.

"What's your name?" I asked after introducing myself.

"Elijah," he replied, greeting me in the name of the Lord.

"Are you a Rastafarian?" I inquired, referring to the religious sect in Jamaica whose members sport matted manes or dreadlocks.

"No," said the stranger, who certainly looked the part.

"Well then, are you an angel?" I asked with a teasing smile.

Elijah paused a moment before he quoted Hebrews 1:14—"Are not all angels God's messengers sent to serve those who will inherit salvation?"

"Very well, you are welcome here, my friend," I said, delighted with this stranger's good-natured wit and peaceful presence.

Elijah said he had no needs and asked nothing of us but Christian fellowship. His voice was kind, his body clean, and his spirit seemed content and connected to God. I always look in people's eyes, the windows of the soul. His were clear, and my spirit was at ease in his presence.

Elijah stayed for Bible study and lived up to his implied vocation as messenger of God. He offered profound insights into the Scriptures, spoke the truth in love, gently admonished a guest who was out of line, and made a positive contribution to the meeting.

Before he left the house, I found out that Elijah once had been a Baptist minister. For the last ten years, however, he has traveled from place to place with a simple bedroll on his back. He hikes cross-country without shirt or shoes, accepting rides if offered. He

LINCOLN CHRISTIAN COLLEGE AND SEMINARY

never asks for food or money, but receives gifts gladly if offered in love. He prefers to sleep outside but enjoys hospitality and a home-cooked meal when God provides.

The secret of his contentment, he says, is in asking himself four questions in every situation:

1. *Am I somewhere I don't need to be?*
2. *Do I need to be somewhere I'm not?*
3. *Do I have something I don't need?*
4. *Do I need something I don't have?*

By honestly facing the answers to these questions, Elijah can either take appropriate action to change the circumstance, or choose to transcend the given situation through prayer and meditation. By embracing simplicity and spiritual discipline, he is free to be God's messenger who blesses those who receive him in love.

Practicing hospitality to strangers, as the Scriptures teach, is the privilege of those who would be friends of God. It requires a simple and generous spirit willing to receive those who come without apparent credentials, and openness to the gifts and lessons they have to offer.

We must also be wise and discerning in our gestures of hospitality, knowing that not all strangers are sent from God. During our open house and hospitality times at the Oak Street House, we sometimes encounter guests who are hostile, disruptive, or downright demonic. We sometimes must ban certain individuals and ask others to leave. Yet most guests are genuinely needy men and women who are blessings in disguise.

Part of the challenge of hospitality is to take the risk,

knowing that tough love is required sometimes and humble recognition of divine presence is required at other times, when we welcome strangers.

Elijah's gift and blessing was in his example of radical dependence on God, challenging us to ask the questions, Am I where I need to be, and what do I really need?

Sometimes I wonder if God doesn't send his angels to us from time to time to remind us that the ministry of hospitality, requiring simplicity and generosity, is at the top of his list.

I know God sent his only begotten Son, who said, "I was a stranger and you welcomed me." The one who had no place to lay his head was welcomed by many who were blessed because of their compassion.

By practicing hospitality, we sometimes welcome not only angels, but the Lord Jesus himself disguised as a poor and nearly naked stranger with a black face, gentle smile, and radiant eyes.

Offering Refuge to the Sojourner

A second strand of biblical teaching on hospitality challenges us to offer refuge to the foreigner in need of protection and provision.

The story of Rahab the harlot is remembered in biblical history as an example of the duty and rewards of extending hospitality to new arrivals in the land. Rahab was the Canaanite who ran a brothel in Jericho and welcomed the two Israelites sent from Joshua to spy out the promised land. When the time came to conquer Jericho, "Joshua spared Rahab the prostitute, with her family and all who belonged to her, because she hid the men Joshua had sent as spies to Jericho" (Josh. 6:25). Both James and the writer of the Letter to the Hebrews call Rahab righteous because of her ministry of hospitality (James 2:25; Heb. 11:31). Matthew's Gospel prologue includes her in the family tree of Jesus as the mother of Boaz, Ruth's husband (Matt. 1:5).

When Israel settled in the land God had given them, the command was to welcome sojourners and offer them a share of what is produced from the land. Those who produce crops must not reap the edges of their field, so that the poor and alien can come and glean what they need to survive (Lev. 19:9, 10). The pilgrim who has left home and become like Moses in Midian, "an alien in a foreign land" (Exod. 2:22), must not be despised, rejected, or mistreated. "The alien living with you must be treated as one of your native-born," God commands his people. "Love him as yourself, for you were aliens in Egypt" (Lev. 19:34).

The biblical teaching is clear: Just as the Lord "defends the cause of the fatherless and the widow, and loves the alien, giving him food and clothing," so are God's people to extend hospitality to those without a home in a foreign land (Deut. 10:18-19).

Decisions to leave one's homeland and family ties are not made easily or without "clear and present danger." That there are approximately ten to fifteen million religious, political, and economic refugees in the world today speaks to the need for compassion and hospitality.

In the past ten years the United States has accepted over one million legal refugees. An estimated two to four million undocumented aliens arrive each year, over half of whom slip through the nets of the United States Immigration and Naturalization Service. Roughly 60 percent of both the legal and illegal immigrants and refugees are Hispanic, a small percentage of whom are granted asylum.[3]

These pilgrims of the world have fled across national borders to escape danger and persecution within their homelands. Some remain in refugee camps without citizenship, some resettle in host countries, and others are forced underground.

God has charged his people with a ministry to the "alien in [their] land." In order to observe the biblical tradition of offering refuge, the church must decide where its loyalty lies—with the state, which requires immigration quotas and due process of law, or with the kingdom, which recognizes no distinction between native and foreign-born.

A test case for Golden Gate Community occurred when a refugee from Nicaragua illegally entered the country and showed up in church on Sunday morning. A few months later, we offered him refuge in our ministry house and committed ourselves to his safety and provision. Part of our journey was to think through the issues of sanctuary and asylum and arrive at a biblical mandate.

A Story of Survival in America

Born to a common family in a poor country where the rich have ruled and the poor have been oppressed for decades, Marcos Cajina grew up believing poverty was nothing to be ashamed of. When he turned twelve, his father discovered that Marcos was not his biological child. Enraged, he threw him out, banishing him to the streets and the mercies of relatives and friends. In 1979, revolution ravaged Nicaragua. Marcos eagerly joined the Sandinistas in their overthrow of the Somoza government and in fighting the contras who opposed the revolution.

After five years of military service, Marcos began to experience a serious health problem. He began to be easily exhausted—an unusual feeling for the lithe, strong young man. Even light activity made his heart race and pound. He was released from duty only to find that the treatment he needed was not available in Nicaragua—or in any nation in Central America.

A North American friend suggested that a visiting delegation of American medical personnel might be able to help. He approached the group, explained his problem, and was examined. A promise was given, along with the name of a San Francisco doctor, that if he found his way to the United States, the necessary tests and the operation he needed would be performed free of charge!

Borrowing, saving, and scraping from every available source, Marcos managed to obtain $204, the fare for a government-approved trip to Mexico City. After arriving there, Marcos walked, hitched rides, and rode a bus to the Texas border. All that now stood between him and the United States was the Rio Grande.

Not knowing where to cross safely, Marcos hired a "coyote"—a Mexican guide who knew the way—for $40. Courageously, he forged the river with arms held overhead to carry the clothes from his back. A Mexican family living on the American side of the border greeted them with the advice to seek refuge and shelter at a sanctuary house in a neighboring town. The only transportation available was a taxi ride for $70!

Refreshed from sleep and food, Marcos left the sanctuary for Houston a few days later. He wanted to continue on his way to San Francisco. Instead of finding directions to California, the police found him. Arrested as an illegal alien, Marcos was thrown into jail the week before Christmas. His crime was being a refugee.

Scores of letters left that Houston jail as Marcos wrote innumerable pleas for help to agencies and officials across the country. One found its way to a medical doctor in San Francisco—the one the North Americans had promised would help Marcos if he found his way to the United States. The doctor was true to his friends' promise; he requested that the Houston authorities release Marcos due to his heart condition. Three months and four days after his arrest, Marcos walked out of the door of the jail without a passport, a Social Security number, or a place to call home. But at least he was free.

With little money in his pockets, he relied on his wits to get to San Francisco. Hitchhiking from Houston to Dallas, somewhere near Austin Marcos's life was spiritually transformed. Sitting in a stranger's car, Marcos began to look back over the last weeks of his life. Each step of the journey had seemed impossible, but somehow he had inched his way to the next place. People he had never met before offered good advice and help. It seemed that a protective, guiding power traveled with him. In those reflective moments, Marcos acknowledged that the God he had ceased to believe in as a child was indeed the One who had repeatedly parted the waters that threatened to overtake him. God was leading him to the promised land of health and safety in San Francisco.

Many Christian people, ranging from Catholic priests and protestant pastors to Salvation Army social workers and hospitable strangers, reached out and helped Marcos cover the final distance from Dallas to San Francisco. He made contact with the doctor who had promised to help him. A series of tests and a heart catheterization was performed. He also was put in touch with the Salvation Army for shelter. Susan Gamboa, the social worker assigned to his case, happened to attend Golden Gate Community and brought Marcos to church.

Susan sat beside Marcos, quietly translating the morning's message on faith. An invitation to come to the table of the Lord was given. His brows furrowed, his lips mouthing silent words, his concentration intense, Marcos knelt to receive Holy Communion for the first time in his life.

After the service concluded, the solemn expression of

the Nicaraguan stranger broke into a smile that bathed his face in a welcoming warmth. Marcos walked immediately into our hearts. A few months later he joined our residency and job development programs. We helped him retain an attorney and encouraged him in the long battle for asylum. Without the church as his refuge, he would not have made it!

Marcos faced two years of deportation proceedings as an undocumented alien. During that time he whole-heartedly embraced the Christian life and graduated from the Oak Street House residential program. In the face of the fact that only 14 percent of Nicaraguan cases for asylum are granted by the court, Marcos's case was a hard one to win. Believing in divine providence, twenty-five concerned friends from the church and mission packed the courtroom in support of their friend.

The atmosphere was tense but hopes were high. Marcos answered all the questions of his lawyer and the district attorney calmly, with conviction, in English. The case hinged on Marcos's change of life, religiously and ideologically, from the years when he had been a revolutionary.

Within an hour, the judge said, "You are granted asylum," and Marcos broke into tears of joy, embracing everyone who had come to court to back his case. A refugee in a foreign land had become a legal resident in a country where he was free.

Later that month Marcos was baptized in the Pacific Ocean as a seal of his faith in Christ. He spoke passionately about the transformation of his life:

"I had to come to the point that I was powerless and that my life was unmanageable. I had to make the decision to turn my will and my life over to God. I needed to be healed. God brought me to the house and into the residential program where I made my transition. . . . After being healed, God also made this promise to me: 'I will make a way for you!' He is now

sending me off to Los Angeles to prepare myself to serve him in his ministry. I ask you to keep me in your prayers as I devote my whole life to God and marry Christ in spirit."

Today, Marcos Cajina lives in Los Angeles and works as an advocate for undocumented immigrants with Las Familias del Pueblo in the garment district of Los Angeles. His goal is to complete his education and become a full-time urban minister. His story is a reminder to all that the Lord is a refuge, and calls his church to be a sanctuary where all are welcomed.

The Church as a Refuge

The biblical mandate to extend hospitality to domestic strangers and foreign pilgrims has nothing to do with whether they are Christian or not. People out of touch with God look to the church for help in time of need. My vision of the urban church is as God's house of refuge.

A refuge is a place of protection and comfort, help and hope, where one is not judged but rather encouraged to learn and grow in the ways of God. As the Statue of Liberty in New York harbor symbolizes, there is a "refuge for the oppressed, a stronghold in times of trouble" (Ps. 9:9). Unlike the guardians of Miss Liberty, however, the Lord does not change divine policy of welcoming the "huddled masses yearning to breathe free." God's arms are always open to the world's refugees, homeless and tempest-tossed. The Lord of liberty stands ready to offer sanctuary and set them free.

This is why God commanded the children of Israel to designate six cities in Canaan as "cities of refuge" under the jurisdiction of priests. These cities were to be places of shelter and safety where a person who was unjustly accused could flee (Num. 35:6).

I believe the church of Jesus Christ, like Israel of old,

is called to be a refuge for the oppressed, a sanctuary for "the least of these." People who are hungry, thirsty, naked, sick, in prison, and alone in an inhospitable land need the church to be a place of protection and provision.

The monastic rule—"Let every guest be received as Christ"— is the ministry ideal at the Oak Street House. Though we do not always live up to our calling, we do record about twelve thousand visits each year, representing over one thousand guests who come repeatedly for hospitality or social services. Runaways, street pilgrims, outcasts, fugitives, and new immigrants have, from time to time, found a place of refuge at the house.

The Oak Street House is open three afternoons and evenings a week for hospitality and an activity. Volunteers receive training and are assigned to a particular afternoon or evening for ministry. A team leader with two assistants is in charge each time and is responsible to the mission director. Community-based ministries hosting drop-in centers may benefit from knowing how the program works for us.

The team prepares for hospitality by showing up a half hour before opening to brew coffee, fix snacks, select music for the desired atmosphere, arrange tables and chairs for convenient conversation, and choose literature for the guests to read.

When the doors are opened to those lined up outside, each guest is warmly greeted and asked to sign in. New guests are informed of the activities and rules of the Oak Street House. Volunteers try to engage guests in conversations to build relationships and identify any problems or needs that should be referred to the staff social worker the following day. Blankets, sleeping bags, food, clothing, and hygiene supplies, which are usually distributed during social service hours, may be given out in emergency situations.

Guests are encouraged to stay for the full two hours of hospitality and invited to the evening activity. The only rule enforced is this: "Remember that this is God's house of prayer, hospitality, and refuge. Nothing should be brought into this house that would disturb its peace and purpose: no smoking, alcohol, or drugs inside; no fighting, verbal abuse, or disturbances will be tolerated; those who have taken a drug or drink today may be asked to leave."

About ten minutes before closing time, guests are informed that the afternoon or evening of hospitality is ending and are encouraged to help clean up. After all guests have gone, the team takes a few minutes to discuss how it went and plan their next time together. Following the meeting, the team leader writes a brief summary of the evening's activities, noting any disturbances, services and referrals made, supplies needed, and other relevant data for the mission director.

Hospitality and Bible Study

Activities, including Bible studies, spiritual direction classes, and Christian entertainment, can easily be incorporated into hospitality times, with redemptive results.

On Wednesday nights at Oak Street House, after the first hour of hospitality, half the guests usually stay for Bible study. We begin by going around the room for "check-in time"; everyone says his or her name and responds to a simple question designed to reveal the state of his or her mind and heart and to lead into the topic of the study. For example, when studying about "perseverance" from Hebrews 12, the opening question might be, "When was the last time you felt like giving up?" Then the scripture text is read aloud, each one reading a verse or two, followed by a teaching and discussion. The hour ends with requests and group prayer in a spirit of unity and concern.

What makes this different from most church Bible

studies is that the members are mostly homeless street folks who believe in God but would not be considered conventional in their religious beliefs and practices. Many are theologically astute, well-read and insightful. Some are hostile toward organized religion yet responsive to a street-level approach to Christian faith.

Every meeting time is unpredictable in the size, spirit, and complexion of the group. Some nights are anointed, while others are plagued by disruptions and spiritual warfare. Often there are outbursts, tangential responses, and disruptions difficult to deal with. The leader must be prepared to hold tight the reins, keep the teaching simple and the discussion focused, and always look for ways to call for spiritual decisions and commitments. At the year's end, we try to determine how many guests experienced Christian conversion or rededication of their lives to the Lord.

It is a real challenge to pastor the homeless and preach the gospel to the poor. Not everyone responds to the ministry of hospitality and the Word, but the opportunity to come to Christ should always be given. Personally, I find it the most rewarding aspect of my mission work, especially when lives are changed.

Gregory's Prayer for Deliverance

Gregory, thirty-one, came to a Wednesday evening Bible study one week primarily for the hospitality that accompanied it. He had attended Sunday school as a child but became a drug addict as a teenager and continued using for twenty years. After the meeting was over, Muriel, one of our staff members, followed up on the spiritual openness that Gregory had expressed during the study. She asked him if she could pray with

111

him and asked me to join them. We formed a prayer circle on the stairs, and Gregory tearfully offered his life to Christ.

After thirty days of sobriety, we encouraged Gregory to apply for residency at the Oak Street House. He had become an out-client at a drug rehabilitation program and was ready for a supportive Christian community. Gregory became a resident, found employment, and viewed his life change as a miracle of God's grace. He was one of six guests that became Christians through the mission Bible study that year.

We extend hospitality and refuge to others so that they will sense God's welcome to the household of faith. Our challenge is to make the sojourner into a guest, a stranger into a friend, a sinner into a saint, in the church and in our homes.

My Home as a Place of Hospitality

The key to hospitality in the home is to welcome a stranger of goodwill the way you would welcome Christ himself if you met him on the road.

Two disciples were walking home on the road to Emmaus when a stranger, who may have looked familiar but who they were kept from recognizing, came up and walked beside them. "What are you discussing?" he asked in a way that revealed his spirit of goodwill.

The two stood still, their faces downcast. "Are you the only one living in Jerusalem who doesn't know what happened?" asked Cleopas in amazement.

"What happened?" asked the stranger.

After telling the story of the death of Jesus and the vision of angels at the empty tomb, the stranger took the lead and opened the Scriptures to them.

As they approached the village where they were going, the stranger acted as if he were going farther. They urged him to join them for a meal and lodging for the night.

Their hospitality was not without reward. When the stranger was at table, he took the bread, gave thanks, broke it, and gave it to them in such a way that their eyes were opened. As soon as they recognized the Lord Jesus, he disappeared from their sight. They were left with burning hearts from his divine presence among them. (Luke 24:13-35, paraphrased)

The rewards of hospitality far outweigh fears, risks, and the need for privacy. Opening your home to strangers opens possibilities for friendship, evangelism, community, and receiving a blessing. Expect a gift from God when you entertain strangers unawares.

Jewish people have a tradition of filling "Elijah's cup," the cup of blessing, at the Passover feast. After prayers are offered for the coming of Elijah, the children are sent to open the door to see if he is coming with a blessing. Everyone is ready to say, "Blessed is he who comes in the name of the Lord."[4]

Another hospitality tradition, resurrected and recommended by Henri Nouwen, is to prepare a "Christ Room" in one's residence, set apart for the stranger or unexpected guest.[5] Mary and Martha literally offered their guest room to Jesus when he retreated from Jerusalem to Bethany. Most of us can prepare a

113

"Christ Room" reserved for Jesus in disguise.

In deciding whether to extend hospitality to domestic strangers and foreign pilgrims, whether in the church or at home, remember this: The stranger has a blessing to offer, but not until he or she becomes a friend; the foreigner brings a message from afar, but not until he or she feels at home. So, fill Elijah's cup and prepare the guest room. One never knows who will come in the name of the Lord.

Notes

1. Henri Nouwen, *Reaching Out* (Garden City, N.Y.: Doubleday, 1975), p. 50.
2. Benedicta Ward, *The Desert Christian* (New York: Macmillan, 1975), p. 25.
3. Otto Friedrich et al., "Immigrants—the Changing Face of America," *Time* 126, no. 1 (July 8, 1985).
4. Ceil and Moise Rosen, *Christ in the Passover* (Chicago: Moody Press, 1978), pp. 84, 85.
5. Henri Nouwen, lecture delivered at Yale Divinity School, Spring 1980.

6

MEETING CITY PEOPLE'S BASIC NEEDS

Starting Food, Shelter, and Clothing Ministries

. . . to share your food with the hungry
and provide the poor wanderer with shelter—
when you see the naked, to clothe him,
and not to turn away from your own flesh and blood?
                                        —Isaiah 58:7

City dwellers live according to their means, whether on the streets or in a penthouse. The hierarchical structure of urban society looks something like this:

Super Rich (penthouse)
Rich (split level home or condominium)
Moderate Income (apartment with a view)
Low Income (ground floor apartment)
Below Poverty (basement level shelter)
Homeless (street level survival)[1]

Since every segment of the population has needs, it becomes important to prioritize basic needs and determine what levels of society you wish to reach.

Most urban ministries, including the one I direct, focus on the basement and street levels of society, which now number three million people. This growing sub-population is comprised of the under-served mentally ill, those supporting substances abuse habits, the poor caught in the generational cycle of poverty, the street-shelter people who drift from place to place, and the "new poor"—those who were productive members of society until recent economic hardships caused them to lose their jobs, their homes, and their self-respect.

The 1987 Conference of Mayors study of twenty-nine cities revealed that one-third of the homeless are families with children, and a large percentage are veterans. The National Institute of Mental Health estimates that as many as one-half of the homeless suffer from a mental illness. The American Psychiatric Association reports that at least 40 percent of the homeless have drug or alcohol dependencies.[2]

The purpose of this chapter is to suggest some simple ways any church or mission group can clothe, feed, and shelter the poor and homeless. Whether you choose to manage a clothing room, start a food program, or become a shelter provider, the principle is the same— *connect resources with needs!*

Managing a Mission Clothing Room and Food Pantry

Providing free clothing, hygiene supplies, and food packs are perhaps the easiest services for a church or mission center to provide. Individuals and other church groups are delighted to donate used clothing and other items if they know of the need. Simply type up a "Material Needs List," send it to your potential supporters, and be prepared to receive an abundance.

Sorting, sizing, and discarding unusable items is the never-ending task of managing a clothing room. No one person can keep pace with the activity; volunteers are needed weekly. Since space is often limited, try to sift out the best clothing and discard the rest.

In stocking the clothing room, the rule is this: Offer what you would proudly wear. What clients generally need and want are casual, natural fiber clothes: jeans,

116

corduroy pants, tennis shoes, walking shoes, jackets, winter coats, belts, gloves, and knit caps. Women need dresses, blouses, undergarments, and scarfs. Polyester items are out, even for street people. Keeping a few dressier items in stock will be appreciated by clients who need aid in preparing for job interviews. There is also a need for children's clothes and sanitary disposable diapers.

After sorting through all your donated clothing, stock what you need and bag up the rest. Goodwill and Salvation Army are happy to take what you cannot use.

Hygiene supplies, such as small disposable samples of soap, shampoo, razors, shaving cream, toothbrushes, toothpaste, deodorant, and facial tissues, are also easily obtained from supporters. Often, people who travel frequently enjoy sending their favorite mission a box of toiletries gathered from hotel visits.

Survival supplies—army or other durable wool blankets, sleeping bags, rain ponchos, and pocket Bibles—are always a premium donation. Food packs containing canned fruits and vegetables, stew meat, rice, beans, macaroni, flour, powdered milk, Malt-o-Meal, peanut butter, and boxes of soup can also be requested from those who want to help. Some of these items, as well as butter and cheese, can be obtained by joining a local food bank servicing churches and nonprofit organizations.

Be sure to acknowledge material donations by a letter or receipt for "goods-in-kind," the value of which is to be determined by the donor.

Distribution of these requested items easily can become chaotic and requires organization and account-ability. Systems need to be thought through and adapted. Records should be kept on what is given out and to whom. There are many procedural options.

Some food and clothing ministries operate by window service: Clients log in and take numbers. When their name or number is called, they go to the window and request clothing by size and food items by need. No browsing is allowed.

Other programs, like the Oak Street House "Benevolence Boutique," encourage clients to shop around and try on items before taking their monthly change of clothes or their food allotment.

Whatever method works best for you, stay with it awhile and work out the bugs. Systematize your policies and procedures and put them in writing. Continue to train volunteers to follow the established procedures, adding quality to your service as it evolves.

Starting a Food Program

Providing food for the hungry may have priority over clothes for the needy. Beyond stocking a food pantry, churches and urban missions can sponsor their own *agape* feasts from time to time, or join together to co-sponsor a neighborhood soup kitchen. Both are effective means of demonstrating your concern.

Generally, groups can do together what they cannot do separately. Golden Gate Community, for example, cooperated with other community organizations and churches to organize the Haight Ashbury Soup Kitchen and the Community Garden for the neighborhood's street population.

It began with one person's dream and a call for co-workers. John Meehan, a local Haight Street personality who still looks and dresses as he did in the sixties, piloted the project. He contacted neighborhood pastors, merchants, and organizational leaders and presented the need and opportunity. He would initially serve as program director, with no salary, and solicit food donations and recruit volunteers, if the rest of us could find a facility and secure equipment and supplies.

The Hamilton United Methodist Church agreed to host the program in their basement, and members of our community became involved in the incorporation process, writing grant proposals, serving as officers on the board of directors, and supplying volunteers.

Today, the Haight Ashbury Soup Kitchen provides quality meals for 250 people a day, four days a week, at a cost to the program of under one dollar per person. It remains a grass-roots effort in which the neighborhood has ownership. After five years of operation, John is still the only paid staff member with a genius for organizing volunteer labor.

A soup kitchen and community garden can be part of any neighborhood if people learn to work together to make it happen.

Another way to feed the hungry, and to do it in style, is to sponsor *agape* feasts. The holidays, especially Thanksgiving, Christmas, and Easter, are especially good times for this kind of special event.

An *agape* feast is simply a banquet given in honor of the poor as a way of expressing divine love for those invited to the Lord's table. It is based on Jesus' instructions to a well-meaning Pharisee who had invited him to his home: "When you give a dinner or a banquet, do not invite your friends or your brothers or your kinsmen or rich neighbors. . . . But when you give a feast, invite the poor, the maimed, the lame, the blind, and you will be blessed" (Luke 14:12-14 RSV).

What a challenge to take these words literally. It is not easy to go out into the streets and alleys of the city and with compassion invite the poor to a social event where they are the honored guests. Yet in so doing we witness to the truth of the great feast of the kingdom prepared for those who respond to the invitation (see Isa. 25:6-8; Luke 14:15-24; Rev. 19:9).

Hosting a first-class banquet for the poor representing the feast of the kingdom serves as a way to communicate to those who feel left out how truly God loves them. For me, the most memorable *agape* feast was the first one I helped organize on Thanksgiving Day in New

York City at the Lamb's Mission, where I was ministering at the time.

Preparations began months in advance as cooks and volunteers were recruited, a menu selected, and invitations printed that read:

> The Honor of Your Presence Is Requested
> at a Banquet at the Lamb's
> Given in Your Honor
> Because of Jesus and His Love

Volunteers and members of the congregation literally went out into the streets and alleys of Times Square and personally invited shopping bag ladies, homeless families, and crippled street folks outside in the cold, as well as residents from the Light House for the Blind, to come to the Lamb's and enjoy Thanksgiving Dinner by the fire. We even rented a black limousine and drove through the city to distribute invitations and offer rides.

We put out our best linen, silverware, and china on round tables in an elegantly decorated ballroom. At 10 A.M. the guests began to arrive, a bit perplexed at the favored treatment they were receiving. They were welcomed at the door and escorted to the second floor facility where a maitre d' in a tuxedo helped them find their seats. A blessing was said, and the feast began. Turkey, ham, fresh salad, homemade pies à la mode—all you could eat—was served with loving attention.

Two hundred invitations had been given out and 150 guests attended the first-class banquet. But why bother with such quality for street people? Why not provide a simple soup line and serve as many poor folks as possible in the shortest amount of time? No invitations, reservations, or accommodations required. The reason for quality and special attention is to make a statement about God's attitude toward the poor. By treating them as honored guests the gospel comes through loud and clear: The Lord favors the poor and oppressed, and desires to bless them and meet their needs!

Musical entertainment was provided during the meal, to which the street people responded with joy and gratitude. One sad old man who probably had not laughed in years started to smile. Before long, he tried to clap to the beat. Others got up from their seats and started to dance. Each guest in his or her own way was visibly moved. Cloudy eyes found clear vision. Cold hearts were strangely warmed. Alienation turned to hope, insecurity to peace, and the harsh realities of street life changed to an experience of comfort and spiritual presence.

Before the banquet ended, I had a chance to verbally share the good news. I read the parable of the feast of the kingdom from Luke 14 and reminded the crowd of this truth: "God Almighty is throwing a banquet, and we're all invited! This feast here today at the Lamb's is only a representation of the one that is to come. It points to and anticipates the heavenly banquet that is prepared for all people. You have all accepted the invitation to come to this Thanksgiving banquet. I hope you will also accept the invitation to God's feast in his kingdom. Jesus says, 'Come, for all things are now ready.' "

While I said all this, a fight broke out in the back, and one of our guests was ushered out. There was more music and sharing. Joe Colaizzi, our host, who got the idea to have the feast from one of Pastor Moore's sermons on the subject, told our guests how they could be spiritually born again. Everyone was quiet as people were invited to come forward to pray. About twenty-five responded. We all prayed.

The man I prayed with had a patch over one eye and had spent many days and nights on the streets. He said he wanted to be saved. The moment I prayed for salvation, his body shook and convulsed. I wasn't sure what was happening. For several minutes he dry-heaved, as if he were throwing up foul spirits lodged so long inside him, making room for the Spirit of God. His nose ran, his mouth salivated, his whole body jerked back and forth. Joe helped me calm him down and asked his name. Finally, he was quiet. George was delivered, cleansed, and reborn.

He came to church the following Sunday calm and sane, hungry for the bread of life. George was received by a congregation who had come to favor God's poor and learned how to welcome them to the Lord's table.

As I reflect on the results of that first *agape* feast in 1977, I would call on churches and missions in every city to welcome into their homes and community centers the hungry and the homeless, the orphans and the widows, the maimed, the lame, and the blind. What a statement it would make about divine love.

Golden Gate Community continues to sponsor a first-class Thanksgiving Feast every year. In 1986, our sister church, Bresee Center Berkeley, organized their first *agape* feast.

Nazarene Church Adopts Rainbow Village

Guess who lives at 2001 Rainbow Junction in Berkeley? Andrew, Zig, Pete, Lance, Hawk, Sapphire, Gemstone, and a host of other "vehicle dwellers" who call Rainbow Village their home.

In 1985, the city granted permission to fifty homeless adults and three children to move their sputtering cars, *vans, trucks, and old school buses to a tiny portion of the Berkeley waterfront next to the city dump. Conditions were primitive—no electricity, heat, telephone, or shower—but the location was preferable to the streets.*

The next year their lease expired, and state authorities would not allow it to be renewed. Faced with forced eviction, most villagers made plans to move. Bresee Center Berkeley, which assisted a Rainbow family at Christmas time with gifts, groceries, and provisions, made a final attempt to reach out in love to several of these folks before evacuation.

On Valentine's Day weekend, the church sponsored a "Love Feast for the Homeless." Church members and villagers mingled as they got to know each other over a spaghetti dinner. Zig was there to play his harmonica. Lance and Pastor Doug Hardy played guitars as everybody sang folk songs and gospel choruses they all knew. Some came early to shower before the feast. Many lingered as they enjoyed a place of refuge in the church.

Seven-year-old Heather from the church sat at the table next to middle-aged Hawk, who sports a pony tail and goatee and is usually shy around people. Yet the two got along famously as they compared notes.

"What's it like to live in your truck?" asked Heather.

"Everybody's got to live somewhere," answered Hawk.

"How do people in Rainbow Village earn a living?" someone wanted to know.

As most of the homeless learn, there are ways to survive. Some sell their blood, some accept charity. Many collect used products that can be recycled. Those with skills and discipline find odd jobs, like Andrew, who sharpens knives for restaurants.

Lively conversation and good times continued until the Love Feast ended. Kenny, the church custodian, sadly remarked, "Now we have to send them back."

123

*Rainbow Village closed the next week. Many called
it a tragedy. Others said, "Good riddance!" Zig, the
official village spokesperson, said that the rise and fall
of Rainbow Village "will give the city something to
remember."*

*At least the villagers would remember that Christ
and his church were a very present help in time of need,
offering a feast during life's stormy weather.*

There are many other ways to feed the hungry besides
soup lines and *agape* feasts: Churches and missions can
form discount food-buying collectives, join a network
food box program, or distribute government surplus
foods. There are "gleaning" ministries in farming areas
that seek distribution centers in the city. There are
"meals on wheels" programs that can be replicated.
With creativity and organization on the part of
inner-city churches and missions, resources can be
connected to needs, the hungry can be fed, and God's
love can be made manifest.

Becoming a Shelter Provider

Just as there are many ways to clothe the needy and
feed the hungry, there are a variety of means to shelter
the homeless. A good way to start is to volunteer at an
existing shelter. This option both provides a service and
allows for a season of testing the waters before plunging
in deeper in providing housing.

If your church or mission has the space and
volunteers, consider hosting a shelter program, or
joining in a community effort to shelter the homeless.
In New York City, 130 churches with limited space
were organized by Here's Life Inner-City to each take
their quota for the night of homeless persons referred
from a central screening service. "Partnership for the

Homeless"—as the cooperative effort is called—is thus able to shelter 1,400 persons in a city with the highest homeless population in the country.

Some urban ministries, like Jubilee Housing in Washington, D.C., sponsored by the Church of the Savior, found a way to purchase medium and large houses with single room occupancy and turn them into "Samaritan Inns." Their vision is to start a thousand inns housing ten thousand people a night.

In San Francisco, Golden Gate Ministries became a neighborhood shelter provider by helping to organize an emergency family shelter. The way the Haight Ashbury Family Shelter was established was similar to how the Haight Ashbury Soup Kitchen started. A dreamer had a dream, and others caught the vision. When the dream was threatened, community churches, city agencies, and individuals rallied to relieve a crisis.

The Saga of a Neighborhood Shelter

What began in the cold winter of 1985, when several of San Francisco's homeless died due to inclement weather, nearly closed a year later when the shelter's funding was depleted.

Hosted by the Hamilton United Methodist Church and assisted by Golden Gate Ministries, the Shelter provided a warm, dry place to sleep; a hot evening meal and breakfast; and assistance in working with Social Services requirements for temporarily displaced single parents, families and expectant couples.

One week before Christmas, an emergency meeting of the board of directors of the shelter was called to manage the crisis. The resigning program director had this report for the board: "Our insurance has expired and we can't pay the new premium; even if we could afford it, our current carrier will no longer insure us. Our bank account has only change in it. The staff have not been paid their meager wage in two months, and we owe the host church money too. Our accounts payable include a $1,400 utility bill, a $240 phone bill, and $400 for janitorial service."

A dozen of us from the neighborhood sat sadly in a circle to consider the options. The chairman of the board wanted to step down. I was elected to replace her, though it was unclear whether we even would be open the next day. The agenda turned to questions of liability and provision.

None of us wanted to avoid liability by closing the shelter or resigning as members. John Meehan, who runs the Haight Ashbury Soup Kitchen, spoke up with passion and said, "This is a church, and we don't want to be in a position on Christmas Eve to have a Mary great with child coming here and have no room in the inn! I say we stay open, with or without insurance, at least until after Christmas, for Christ's sake!"

Edrea and Kimberly, the shelter supervisors, were willing to continue working without pay at least a few more days. And there was encouragement from Dr. Steve Thompson, the host pastor, to try to keep going. We voted to find a new insurance carrier, look to outside help, and not to close.

Considerable interest was stimulated by a newspaper feature entitled "Church That Helps the Homeless Could Use Some Help." A photographer had showed up one night and shot pictures of Mrs. Morris and her five children sleeping on floor mats, her babies in shopping carts. The story that ran with the photos described the plight of the homeless as Christmas approached:

"Fifty people a night, most of them women with young children, are sleeping on mats at the Waller

Street church. 'More and more often we're seeing families with three, four . . . or five kids. They're the new poor, the people who find it hardest to rent a place in San Francisco' said the director."[3]

Funds trickled in following the feature, and pressure came to bear on the Mayor's office. City social services responded by providing for the insurance premium. Students and faculty from the University of San Francisco who heard about the need took up a Christmas collection and helped us pay the utility bill. Generous individuals and churches donated what they could. An enthusiastic board and a highly motivated staff worked hard to connect resources with needs.

On Christmas Eve the shelter was open. Edrea was on duty, decorating the basement for Christmas. The residents were busily opening presents, trying on clothes, and playing with toys donated that day by local merchants. There was a festive mood at midnight when I arrived with a Christmas tree that had been given to the shelter.

Edrea told me a young woman with her two-month-old baby had just arrived, and they were out of blankets. I happened to have a blanket in my car and offered it to mother and child. Suddenly, I remembered John's prophecy at the board meeting the week before: "We don't want to be in a position on Christmas Eve to have Mary great with child coming here and have no room in the inn!"

The homeless really understand Christmas, I thought. To them it means that Mary had no place to lay her head, so she found a shelter, wrapped her baby up in a blanket, and laid him in a shopping cart.

After the holidays, the board met again. This time we were able to pay our staff their back salaries. A new program director was appointed and annual funding secured. We could not help but give thanks for the resurrection of a shelter at Christmastime.

127

Offering Whatever Gifts We Have

A church or mission may not have the means to organize or manage a neighborhood soup kitchen or shelter, but there is always something that can be done to alleviate the suffering of the homeless. At the very least, churches and missions can acquire and distribute sleeping bags and blankets to the homeless population. Having blankets and bags on hand at a mission center ensures that those who must sleep in the parks and on the streets are not turned away empty handed when they knock on your door. As Mother Teresa says, "I am only one, but I am one. I cannot do everything, but I can do something."

One thing urban Christians can do is occasionally walk the streets or venture into the parks. When you see a homeless man or women trying to sleep uncovered, offer them a sleeping bag or blanket in Jesus' name. This is the approach of young Trevor Ferrell of Philadelphia, who made "blanket runs" his ministry in the city.

Trevor's Campaign for the Homeless

In 1983, Trevor, age eleven, was enjoying Christmas with his family when a television news special on the homeless caught his eye.

"Do people really live like that?" he asked his father. Trevor's dad, Frank, assured him that people did indeed live on the streets in downtown Philadelphia only a dozen miles from their comfortable suburban home.

"Well, can we go downtown and help them?" Trevor asked pointedly.

128

"Why not!" Frank answered, expecting his son's compassionate impulse to quickly be replaced by another whim. But Trevor, who had read about the good Samaritan in Sunday school, persisted: *"How 'bout tonight!"*

His parents consented to drive him downtown with his pillow and yellow blanket to see the homeless. They drove through a number of streets and spotted a man sleeping on a steamy subway grate, trying to keep warm. Trevor offered the man his blanket and said, *"God bless you."* The man smiled and returned the blessing.

That one night in the winter of 1983 changed the Ferrell family forever. Their involvement mushroomed from reaching out to one huddled man at Christmas to over 120 people nightly. The *"blanket runs"* continued as friends and neighbors donated to *"Trevor's Campaign for the Homeless."*

As the campaign caught on, more and more people wanted to help. Frank finally quit his job to administer his son's ministry. His wife Janet started a thrift store for the needy. A thirty-three room downtown hotel that required renovation was donated to the campaign, and *"Trevor's Place"* was founded as a home for the homeless. A year later a book was in print: Trevor's Place: The Story of the Boy Who Brings Hope to the Homeless.[4]

Today, there are a dozen local chapters of Trevor's Campaign in cities around the world, inspiring thousands to do what they can. *"I fell in love with that little boy named Trevor,"* said a street person who had lost his own wife and son, *"and at the same time, I fell in love with life."*

Offering tangible services in the form of clothing, food, and shelter, or even a blanket, not only demonstrates God's love in action, but fulfills the ancient prophecy and brings a blessing:

129

Is not this the kind of fasting I have chosen:
 to loose the chains of injustice
· ·
Is it not to share your food with the hungry
 and provide the poor wanderer with shelter—
when you see the naked, to clothe him,
 and not to turn away from your own flesh and blood?
Then your light will break forth like the dawn,
 and your healing will quickly appear;
then your righteousness will go before you,
 and the glory of the LORD will be your rear guard.
Then you will call, and the LORD will answer;
 you will cry for help, and he will say: Here am I.
(Isa. 58:6-9)

Notes

1. Diagram is adapted from Gordon Cosby's pamphlet, *On Behalf of the Crushed and Needy* (Washington, D.C.: The Church of the Savior, 1985), p. 2. Used by permission of publisher.
2. Barbara Boxer, "Update on Housing and the Homeless," *Special Report from Barbara Boxer, Member of Congress, Sixth District, California* (February 1988).
3. "Church That Helps the Homeless Could Use Some Help," *San Francisco Chronicle*, December 5, 1986.
4. Frank and Janet Ferrell, *Trevor's Place: The Story of the Boy Who Brings Hope to the Homeless*, with Edwin Wakin (San Francisco: Harper & Row, 1985).

7

MEETING CITY PEOPLE'S SPECIAL NEEDS

Assisting Alcoholics, Drug Abusers, and the Mentally Disabled

God, Grant me the serenity to accept the things I cannot change, the courage to change the things I can, and the wisdom to know the difference. —Reinhold Niebuhr

City people have special needs that can be met, beyond food, clothing, and shelter: Spiritually, people need to know God loves them and can make them whole; emotionally, people need to be supported, encouraged, and loved; those with dependencies need release; the psychologically distraught need healing.

Compassionate ministries address the total needs of city people, beginning with the temporal and penetrating to the needs of the spirit. The purpose of this chapter is to focus on the dependent, distraught, and neglected groups who fall in the cracks of the church, namely, (1) alcohol abusers, (2) drug abusers, and (3) the mentally ill.

Alcoholics

As many as one in ten people in your church or mine are dealing with problem drinking. In urban missions,

131

the majority of clients will be substance abusers. We need to know the nature of the disease, how to confront it, and how to point the way to healing. Let us begin by looking at the disease called alcoholism.

These facts are commonly known:

- Three ounces of alcohol can relax you, while thirty ounces can kill you. Ingesting quantities in between can cause a variety of problems.
- Alcohol indirectly accounts for at least 10 percent of all deaths and is the third major health problem in the United States today.
- Alcohol is known to be involved in over half of all traffic fatalities, crimes, suicides, homicides, accidents, and family violence.
- Two out of every three adults drink. One in ten people who drink will become alcoholic.
- Alcoholism affects not only the abuser but also family, employer, and friends. Forty to sixty percent of children of alcoholic parents will become alcoholics themselves.

The American Medical Association defines alcoholism as "an illness characterized by preoccupation with alcohol and loss of control over its consumption."[1] Alcoholics Anonymous, widely acknowledged as the most successful program available, describes alcoholism as a "disease of denial." The lie is "I can cope with a drink."

For alcoholics, use that relieves stress turns to abuse that alters reality. In time, a dependency is formed, and addiction eventually takes over. When the point of addiction has been reached, the alcohol level must be maintained within the bloodstream in order to avoid painful withdrawal. The process of deterioration sets in, culminating finally in sickness, confinement, or death.

Alcoholism is a disease with distinguishing characteristics. Contrary to the image, the typical alcoholic is not the down-and-out skid row drunk demanding a handout. Street alcoholics only account for about 3 percent of all alcoholics. More likely, the respectable person sitting next to you in church is struggling with the disease and will probably die from it if help is not obtained.

Alcohol is the most commonly abused substance, but anything can be abused: money, power, food, drugs, emotions, sex, relationships. What can be said about those who abuse alcohol can be applied to all compulsive personalities and addictive behaviors. And the path that leads to healing is the same for all substance abusers: (1) hitting bottom and admitting to powerlessness, (2) finding help from God, and (3)committing to life change. The road to recovery is not a solitary one but is facilitated by (4) confrontation and support from others.

Hitting Bottom

Alcoholics Anonymous, with 676,000 members, has over the past fifty years developed principles of recovery based on the lessons of experience. It is difficult to improve upon the Twelve Traditions and Twelve Steps of AA. Over fifty million people have recovered through AA since it began in 1935, and 50 percent of those who attend AA meetings never drink again.

The first step of AA describes "hitting bottom": "We admitted we were powerless over alcohol—that our lives had become unmanageable."

It is never easy to admit defeat, but when a person finally hits bottom and gives up denial, a healing process begins. It is a paradox of both faith and recovery that strength is found in admitting weakness. Alcoholics must face the unmanageability of their disease and the dark reality of their condition. The way up from rock bottom begins with detoxification and the realization that "I am powerless; I have come to the end of my rope!"

Alcohol detoxification refers to a three to five day process during which the body rids itself of alcohol toxins. Withdrawal is a painful process involving anxiety, trembling or shaking, severe perspiration, tingling or crawling of the skin, unquenchable thirst, nausea, and frequent vomiting. It is also possible that "detox" will result in life-threatening convulsions or terrifying hallucinations (called "the DTs"). Withdrawal from alcohol is more dangerous than withdrawal from heroin.

A medically supervised detox, in which a doctor monitors and manages some of these symptoms, is preferable. But it is usually not available to patients without money or insurance. A "cold turkey" detox under supervision usually is not physically harmful unless a person has medical problems, in which case detoxification can be fatal.

Most cities have treatment programs and detox centers that accept both insured and non-insured patients. If you are dealing with someone who has hit bottom and needs to detoxify, try to get him or her into a residential program, and give support through the process.

Help from a Higher Power

Step two of the AA Twelve Steps program states: "Came to believe that a Power greater than ourselves could restore us to sanity."

If a destructive power greater than ourselves nearly destroyed us, perhaps another power greater than ourselves can save us. It is the undeniable experience of

AA members that there is a Higher Power whose strength replaces their weakness, whose healing power restores their sanity, and who leads them into the process of restoration.

Most AA members have faith in God as the Higher Power. Others seem to experience God as the Higher Power without recognizing the Lord as personal Savior. Some even identify the Higher Power with their own inner resources, with their spiritual selves, or with AA itself. What is essential for healing to happen is for God to respond to a mustard seed of faith, however limited, and for the person to commit to a spiritual path that leads to wholeness.

Committing to Life Change

Alcoholics need not understand all about God before God can be a very present help in time of trouble. They need only commit to the Power and the process of recovery.

After the first seventy-two hours of detoxification, approximately twenty-five more days are needed for the body to be free from all toxins associated with alcohol. Commitment to residential treatment is critical at this stage. After the first month, the recovering alcoholic needs to commit to a program of sobriety offering daily accountability.

Participants of AA report that it takes a full year to recover physically and psychologically from alcohol abuse. There may be critical days along the way—three months, six months, and eleven and a half months after detoxification—characterized by agitated states or preoccupation with drinking. These crisis moments are high-risk occasions requiring special precautions and support.

Finally, the fog begins to clear and from then on, it's "easy does it—one step at a time," for recovery is a lifelong process of following the steps: (1) "I can't"; (2) "God can"; (3) "I choose to let him!"

Lead Me to the Rock That Is Higher Than I

My friend Robert did not hit bottom until after ten years of heavy drinking, when he got drunk and nearly died of hypothermia in the park. Upon waking, he found himself in the hospital and submitted to a detox program. Even that rock-bottom experience was not deep enough for his recovery to be sustained.

The following year, we found Robert collapsed under the backyard porch of our mission center. Unconscious, half naked, with the evidence of many hours of sickness and delirium caked on his body, we dumped him into the back of a Mobile Assistance patrol van bound for the detox center. This time, hitting bottom was a major step toward recovery.

Robert submitted to treatment, joined an AA program, committed himself to life change, and found a "Higher Power" to help him stay sober. Every day he went to AA meetings until his craving for alcohol was replaced with a stronger desire for health and wholeness.

After several months of sobriety, Robert came back to church. It surprised me that he knelt to receive communion. I felt compelled to lay my hands upon him and pray that God would save and heal him. "You can't make it on your own, Robert," I prayed. "Let Jesus help you!"

As he testified after the service, he came to recognize the "Higher Power" of AA as Jesus Christ, the all-powerful friend to those who are weak. We gave Robert a certificate of new life and became part of his support group. That was in 1984. He has enjoyed sobriety ever since.

Confrontation and Support

You cannot stop a person from drinking himself or herself to death, but you can confront and support the alcoholic in taking steps toward sobriety.

Confrontation is the process of challenging an alcoholic's minimizing, rationalizing, and denial of behavior. Confrontation does not have to be oppressive, but it must be honest. Without strong feedback and reminders from those who care, the alcoholic sees no alternative but to continue in the disease and believe lies about himself and others.

The worst way to "help" an alcoholic is to make excuses for the behavior, to rescue the "victim," or to be drawn in as a "co-dependent." Playing the enabling role serves only to spread the sickness, making alcoholism a family disease.

The best way to help is to speak the truth in love: Mirror back inappropriate behavior; refuse to give in to demands for attention; avoid being manipulated or taken in by promises; convey acceptance of the person without condoning behavior; listen but do not commiserate. Do not take care of the alcoholic as a parent would a child, for it only feeds the disease. Resist the tendency to threaten, moralize, or preach. Instead, be firm, fair, and consistent. Do what you say you will do. As painful as it is to watch, let the alcoholic hit bottom—whatever that means for him or her. Lay responsibility and the consequences of behavior sharply where they belong: not on the abused substance but on the abuser!

Confrontation is simply the expression of "tough love" that endures the initial, angry outbursts of an addictive personality by focusing on the absolute need for that person to seek recovery. It can be accomplished

137

by family members, friends, employer, church members, or staff members at the mission where the alcoholic knows he or she is loved. Confrontation, however, is only the first step. Recovery is a long, hard road of "hitting bottom" and slowly climbing back up.

Drug Abusers

Alcohol is the most common substance of abuse; psychoactive drugs follow closely behind. Obsessive-compulsive tendencies are common to both types of abusers. What has been said about recovery from alcohol can be applied to recovery from drug addiction. Nevertheless, the world of drugs requires special knowledge and intervention guidelines. This section, though technical, merely scratches the surface.

The World of Drugs

In dealing with drug addicts, it helps to have a general, working knowledge of the three major drug families: (1) depressants, (2) stimulants, and (3) hallucinogens or psychedelics.

1. *Depressants* include alcohol, narcotics, barbiturates, and other sedatives. They depress the central nervous system and decrease its ability to respond to stimuli.

Narcotics such as heroin, morphine, and codeine, also called "opiates," are produced from the opium poppy and along with the synthetically produced narcotics Demerol and Percodan are properly used to reduce pain in cases of severe medical need. They are abused by those who seek anxiety relief and induced euphoria. Narcotics can be injected or taken orally and are physically addictive. A pure narcotic overdose can kill. Combined use with alcohol is also life-threatening. Withdrawal is painful but not fatal.

Barbiturates have a hypnotic effect similar to alcohol.

Phenobarbital, Seconal ("Red Devils"), Tuinal ("Rainbows"), and Nembutal ("Yellow Jackets") are sometimes prescribed as sleeping pills or muscle relaxers, but are all too often abused. Physically addictive, these drugs depress the central nervous system and can be fatal if taken in large quantities. A person who has overdosed will need to be hospitalized immediately. Withdrawal without medical supervision can be fatal.

Tranquilizers are anxiety reducing, muscle relaxing sedatives. Miltown, Librium, and Valium are commonly prescribed and commonly abused. Their effects are similar to those of the barbiturates, but reduced in intensity. The dangers of withdrawal are somewhat less pronounced.

2. *Stimulants* are a family of drugs that include amphetamines and cocaine. They are used to stimulate the central nervous system and produce heightened activity. (Yes, caffeine is also a stimulant and is found in coffee, tea, most soft drinks, and even chocolate!)

Amphetamines are chemically structured after the body's natural stimulant, adrenaline. Benzedrine, dexedrine, and methedrine, commonly known as "pep pills" or "speed," have the effect of postponing fatigue, suppressing appetite, bolstering energy, and intensifying sexual feelings. Commonly abused, "speed" produces a state of agitation and hyperactivity that can lead to amphetamine psychosis, with symptoms similar to the psychological disorder called paranoid schizophrenia. After the drug wears off, the physical and psychological effects can be devastating. The user may suffer extreme lethargy, anxiety, depression, disorientation, and suicidal states of mind. Amphetamines are both physically and psychologically addictive. Withdrawal is physically painful but not life-threatening.

Cocaine, like amphetamines, is a stimulant. It increases the heartbeat and breath rate, raises body temperature and blood sugar levels, and dilates the pupils. Extracted from the leaves of the coca plant,

139

cocaine has become the drug of choice to an estimated five million Americans. Use of its purest form, "crack," is on the rise faster than any other drug. Cocaine can be taken in many different forms: chewed, smoked, injected, drunk, inhaled as powder, or breathed as vapor. The pleasurable effects of cocaine last twenty to thirty minutes, but a person can die of cocaine suffocation. In one recent year, overdoses of cocaine resulted in at least three hundred deaths in the United States.[2]

3. *Hallucinogens* are a psychedelic, "mind-expanding" family of drugs. They include LSD (a synthetic compound made in laboratories), psilocybin (derived from mushrooms), and peyote (containing mescaline, from the seed pods of the Mexican mescal cactus). They are also known as hallucinogens because they alter brain activity and cause hallucinations—internally produced sense perceptions, otherworldly sensations, and intensified feelings. "Tripping" can also result in panic, paranoia, and flashbacks. A person in such a state can be "talked down" or given a "map" by an experienced listener who accepts the user's concept of "reality," reassures him along the way, and protects him from physical danger. Hallucinogens are psychologically, but not physically, addictive. Extended use is known to have harmful effects, such as impaired judgment, lethargy, and psychotic reactions. Repressed behavior is often acted out under the influence of psychedelics.

The Addictive Process

It is my conviction, which is shared by others, that alcoholism, chemical dependency, co-dependency, food disorders, and other obsessive-compulsive behaviors (including gambling and sexual promiscuity) are all outgrowths or manifestations of a basic addictive process.[3]

The addictive process may be genetically based or be the result of early childhood experiences. It surfaces with experimentation and enjoyment of particular substances or activities. Underlying difficulties or disorders invite a casual user to escape through habitual use. Physical or psychological tolerance for the substance increases a user's desire for more. A habit of devotion becomes a religion of dependence. Denial and fantasy set in, allowing a user to say or do anything to get the substance or to participate in the behavior he or she craves. Conscience, truth, reason, and prudence are distorted beyond clear vision. As with alcoholism, deterioration takes over and the process leads to personal destruction.

What is addiction, then? In physical terms, it is dependence on any substance your body craves and can't seem to live without; in psychological terms, anything you organize your life around, become obsessed with, or are compulsive about. In moral terms, it is anything you feel you have to lie about. In theological terms, it is any idol you worship or any besetting sin that's got you hooked. (For a metaphorical illustration of addiction, read Job 41 about struggling with the dragon called Leviathan!)

The addictive process is subtle and deadly. As the ancient proverb reminds us, "The snake you kiss eventually strikes you!" Once addicted to its venom, nothing short of a miracle of intervention and deliverance can reverse the addictive process that leads to physical, psychological, and spiritual death.

Intervention Principles and Drug Counseling

When a person addicted to drugs stops using, he or she goes through the painful withdrawal syndrome, during which the body detoxifies and adjusts to the removal of the drugs. Common withdrawal symptoms include

141

increased blood pressure, severe cramps, anxiety attacks, irritability, and restlessness. Before and after this process, drug counseling and intervention techniques are needed.

Some drug counseling situations will require crisis intervention, either over the telephone or face to face. In such cases, keep these principles in mind:

1. Act calmly, with self-confidence. You are the drug abuser's contact with reality. You need to find a way to empower the person to make a positive choice.

2. Find out what drugs and quantities have been taken. Determine if medical attention is necessary based on your knowledge of the drugs and information you can gain from others.

3. Confront the person if necessary by simply saying, "Back off, cool off, and take a look at what you're doing!" Do not minimize, rationalize, or otherwise enable drug-induced behavior.

4. Do not get into arguments. Do not moralize. Answer only questions being raised. Deal with the person's anxiety. Draw out the person's feelings. Explore what the person intends to do about the situation.

5. If a user desires to stop using, determine if the withdrawal will require medical supervision. If so, get the person into a professional program. If the choice is "cold turkey," prepare the person for a week or more of hell. Find an ex-addict who has been through the experience to stay by the person's side.

It is important to remember that substance abuse is a symptom of a set of underlying difficulties that have become unmanageable. Success does not happen overnight. Recovery is a way of life. The real problem is a compulsive personality and the addictive process.

As with alcoholics, so with all addicts—admitting "I can't do it on my own," realizing "God can help me," and committing to the process of life change are prerequisites for recovery. Those who confront the drug abuser, offering tough love, acceptance, and forgiveness as well as support and accountability, can be effective in intervention.

An ex-addict on the road to recovery will need to commit to at least four major life changes: (1) embracing a new, drug-free environment where old relationships and familiar temptations are minimized; (2) redirecting energy and replacing negative behaviors with positive ones; (3) finding one's place in a faith community or other support group, knowing that one cannot make it alone; and (4) committing to a daily recovery program such as the Twelve Steps of Alcoholics or Narcotics Anonymous. If these four changes are accomplished in the course of a year or two, sobriety will continue as a day-by-day opportunity to grow. If any of these opportunities for change are avoided, recovery will be slower in coming.

Frank's Road to Recovery

My friend Frank, age thirty-one, is a recovering drug addict. He was raised in a conservative Christian home by devout parents who took him to church for Sunday school, Sunday morning worship, Sunday night,

Wednesday night, and every time there was an evangelist in town.

When Frank turned fifteen, his mother died, and it was then that he started to get into trouble. For the next fifteen years, he tried every drug he could find and eventually became addicted to heroin. After several suicide attempts, Frank ended up in a VA hospital under heavy methadone treatment. The program was not effective.

When he found his way to the Oak Street house, Frank was at the end of his rope. We took him in, prayed with him for healing and deliverance, and supported him through detoxification. He made a strong commitment to Christ and found Christian community to be a healing balm. Frank became a new person, made friends easily, attended services regularly, and assisted in the mission.

After eleven and a half months of Christian commitment, a perfect record of chemical freedom, and a stable track record as a resident and volunteer, Frank suffered a relapse. We kicked him out, and he was on the streets again.

Through professional counseling, Frank managed to deal with some underlying difficulties and internal conflicts. He slowly regained his faith and returned to the mission, which embraced him.

Frank's story is not over, but he found his place of love and healing in the church. His experience illustrates that recovery takes time, that there is a journey and a process in finding health and wholeness, and that a supportive community is essential to healing.

The Mentally Disabled

Substance abuse is not the only life-controlling problem affecting the quality of life. Mental illness is a fact of life in the city: A bag lady sits in her usual spot and talks incessantly to herself; a street preacher rants and raves at those who pass by; a derelict strutting down the street shouts obscenities for no apparent reason; a little old man sits silently on a park bench, unresponsive to human interaction.

These are familiar scenes in most cities. By some estimates, as much as 50 percent of the homeless population is mentally disabled. Deinstitutionalization of the chronically mentally disabled is largely the cause for the large numbers of psychiatric patients walking the streets.

In the past twenty-five years, the patient population in mental hospitals decreased by 65 percent. The idea was for community health clinics, halfway houses, and residential care units to help integrate the mentally disabled population into public life. But the idea did not work. Thousands fell through the cracks in the system and were left to survive the best they could.

Stressful setbacks and life on the streets over an extended time also can cause otherwise normal personalities to go over the edge. As Jesse Jackson said at an Oakland rally for the homeless, after he was interrupted by a mentally disabled shelter client, "Take away a person's home, and it will blow his mind!"

All aspects of society are affected by the problem. It tears families apart; confronts our moral sensitivities; fuels ethical and legal debates; drains the resources of existing social services, mental health programs, and housing programs; and challenges the urban church.

Urban churches and city missions automatically attract the mentally disabled to their services and programs. Beyond offering love and acceptance, little can be done for this group. It helps to know the symptoms of mental illness so that tolerance instead of anger can be directed toward those who sometimes act inappropriately.

A staggering 29.4 million Americans suffer from a

psychological disorder![4] Traditionally, mental health professionals have divided psychological disorders into two main groupings: neuroses and psychoses. Labels change, but for simplicity's sake, let us briefly identify the disorders of each.

Neuroses are characterized by uncontrollable anxiety, fears, depressions, and obsessions. Sometimes these are due to a chemical imbalance in the brain. At other times they are due to childhood traumas and life experiences. Though these disorders affect one's quality of life, they do not usually involve a loss of contact with reality. Panic attacks, phobias, and obsessive-compulsive behaviors are examples of neuroses.

Psychoses are disorders that do involve a loss of contact with reality. Schizophrenia is the term applied to severe cases of delusion, disturbed thought processes, bizarre feelings, and uncontrollable behavior. Schizophrenia affects approximately 1 percent of the American population and accounts for roughly half the patients confined to mental institutions. The disease is also found among city people on city streets.

Schizophrenia has easily recognizable characteristics. Persons may appear withdrawn, unresponsive to what is going on around them, and into their own unique time and space. They may display unusual motor behavior ranging from frenzied excitement to complete immobility or a catatonic state. They may react with inappropriate emotions or entertain delusions of grandeur (believing themselves to be Jesus Christ) or paranoia (believing others are conspiring against them).

With proper medication, most mentally disabled persons are manageable and responsive to spiritual truth. A man I call "King Fisher," for example, is our most faithful church attender and Bible study participant. His knowledge of the Scriptures, church history, and the etymology of words is staggering. He loves God and prays for others. But without his medication, King Fisher is wacko!

One time when he got evicted from his residential care unit, King Fisher went without his medication for a week on the streets. Though out of control, he managed to call the mission from a pay phone. His message required deciphering: "The well doesn't go to the thirsty; the thirsty goes to the well. Send an emissary to Haight Street." We sent our social worker to Haight Street to find him and assess the situation. King Fisher needed his medication. We got him admitted to a crisis center, and they found him a new residential program. He stabilized and returned to church and mission activities the following week as though nothing had happened.

I recall another encounter with a mentally disabled person that did not turn out as well. An unruly man walked into church service a half hour late. As he approached me at the pulpit, I knew we were in trouble. He started yelling at the top of his lungs: "Hypocrites! Serpents! Brood of vipers! Who do you think you are!" Our usher was too shocked or afraid to try to stop him. The deluded man declared himself to be Jesus Christ and then proceeded to baptize me and others with spittle from his mouth. I managed to remove him from church myself, making the sign of the cross in front of him as I backed him out the door.

Both neurotic and psychotic disorders are common and treatable. Therapy can help and inner healing is possible. However, patience and a willingness to deal with people who live in a different reality are required, as Stephen's story illustrates:

Stephen in the Snake Pit

There was no way he would miss the annual event. For weeks he had looked forward to Golden Gate

Community's third anniversary. After two and a half years of faithful church attendance, his conspicuous absence caused us alarm. All day, people wondered where he was.

The phone jangled on Tuesday morning. An uncharacteristically serious and humorless voice reported, "I'm back in the snake pit."

"What happened?" I asked.

"I was minding my own business when two cops took me by surprise. They insisted I get in the car. Before I knew it, it was good-bye San Francisco. . . ."

I immediately contacted the social worker assigned to his case. I discovered that my friend, Stephen, whom I had once saved from being stabbed in his hotel, had escaped three years ago after spending fourteen years in the state psychiatric hospital. Little did I know when I met him that my religious friend was a fugitive.

Known in the Tenderloin neighborhood as "the Preacher," he began attending services after we met him in the park during a gospel outreach concert. He made his presence known by singing and dancing to the music and by running around in circles like a madman.

His behavior became less erratic and more sociable over the months of association with the church and mission. At every service he prayed for the poor, sick, and imprisoned. He called us daily at the office to report on the "atmosphere" of the streets. Often he would accompany me on speaking engagements to give his testimony.

A friend to everyone he met, including drug pushers and prostitutes, the Preacher spent his days, as he put it, "helping people transform their ways over to God." Now he was back in the "psych ward," serving time again for an assault charge from his younger days.

My wife and I went to encourage our friend during this time of need. Upon entering the huge, seventeen building state hospital, we learned that a total population of 1,750 mental patients in fifty wards *spends its time here. The hospital's reputation varies between an exemplary social institution and a snake pit, depending on who is describing it.*

When we finally located him, it angered me to see him locked up behind door after door, corridor after corridor, in a ward with padded walls. While we visited him, we were interrupted several times by other patients exhibiting extreme psychotic behavior.

"These people are nuts!" I exclaimed to Stephen as we moved into the screened-in conference room. "We gotta get you out of here!"

"I hear you, partner," he said. "What're we gonna do?"

"First thing is for you to file a petition for your case to be reviewed in court," I said. "If all goes well and your doctor agrees, I'm told you'll be out in two to three weeks."

The Preacher was reluctant to sign any papers. The system had not been kind to him before. The last time he had signed papers he had been confined for life to psychiatric care and shot full of Thorazine (a very potent tranquilizer) to keep him under control. No way would he sign any more papers. "Being paranoid," he reminded me, "does not mean that they are not out to get you!"

Weeks later, Stephen agreed to sign the necessary papers that would be filed as a petition for his case to be reviewed. The unresolved felony charge from twelve years past complicated a simple release. His hearing finally came and lasted for three days. I was prepared to testify in his behalf and was able to make a statement to the judge in court. Several church members appeared in court in support of the Preacher.

Miraculously, all charges were dismissed. The Preacher was released from custody, discharged from the hospital, and officially restored to sanity. His friends in the courtroom applauded the verdict and congratulated him. The Preacher himself was over-

149

come with joy and excitement. Our ride back to San Francisco was quiet and reflective. It was hard for Stephen to believe that the years of institutionalization and fugitive existence were over.

Proudly he showed off his discharge papers to friends in the city. After staying at the Oak Street House that first weekend, he was able to rent a room downtown. But paranoia again set in, and he escaped.

Today, the Preacher roams the streets of the city, ranting and raving at those who have no regard for the homeless and, in his own way, helping people "transform their ways over to God."[5]

Let the Healing Waters Flow

Why do we tend to believe that healing comes easily to those who believe? Are alcoholics instantly cured when they come to Christ? Does an addictive personality suddenly find release from drugs? Do paranoid schizophrenics automatically find sanity when they pray to God? Does a person with a history of sabotaging relationships learn commitment overnight?

Without denying God's power to save and heal, there are few miracles of instantaneous deliverance in my experience in the city. If it takes a person twenty years to hit bottom, it may take at least half that long to overcome destructive patterns, even with God's help. Sins can be forgiven in an instant, attitudes can change overnight, but habit patterns can take years to replace.

The church is sometimes impatient with a weak Christian's rate of progress and judgmental of those who suffer setbacks along the way. It has been said many times that the church is the only army in the world that shoots its wounded. That is to say, stronger Christians sometimes expect too much and are quick to pull the trigger rather than taking the time to offer healing balms to those who hurt.

This is especially true in dealing with difficult cases: the fringe people who can't seem to get their act together or who have problems that never seem to go away. The church either ignores them, blames them for lack of faith, or tolerates them in patronizing ways. We need to learn that though the Lord "heals all thy diseases," it doesn't happen overnight. "By his stripes we are healed" implies no easy deliverance, but an invitation to share in Christ's suffering as well as victory.

Jeremiah had a haunting indictment for priests and prophets in Israel:

> They dress the wound of my people
>   as though it were not serious.
> "Peace, peace," they say,
>   when there is no peace.
>
> (Jer. 8:11)

I've been guilty at times of giving people what has been called "the once-over-lightly prayer." Offering superficial blessings or believing in fast cures constitutes a "light healing." Taking scripture verses out of context and carelessly applying them to people's issues is to "dress the wound of my people as though it were not serious." And saying "Peace, peace," when there are deep disturbances making it obvious that "there is no peace" is dishonesty in ministry. This, I believe, is what the prophet Jeremiah condemns in religious leaders and caregivers.

But there is a river whose streams are meant to bring peace and healing to the people of God (Ps. 46:4). According to the prophetic imagination, the river of God flows from the temple of God through cities and into the sea. As it flows, its clear, crystal water brings life to swarms of living creatures. And the trees along the riverbank bear fruit for food and leaves for the healing of nations (Ezek. 47:1-12; Rev. 22:1-2).

151

In the present age, there will always be those with special needs that never seem to go away. But the day is approaching when perfect healing will come. According to the Christian vision, "the throne of God and of the lamb will be in the city." On that day, the curse will be lifted and God's healing light will shine on all. "He will wipe every tear from their eyes. There will be no more death or mourning or crying or pain, for the old order of things has passed away" (Rev. 21:4; 22:3-5). *Maranatha*—come quickly Lord, to save and heal!

Notes

1. Lewis J. Lord et al., "Coming to Grips with Alcoholism," *U.S. News and World Report* 103, no. 22 (November 30, 1987): 59.
2. Zick Rubin and Elton B. McNeil, *Psychology: Being Human* (New York: Harper & Row, 1985), p. 84.
3. Melody Beattie, *Co-dependent No More* (San Francisco: Harper & Row, 1987).
4. Rubin and McNeil, *Psychology: Being Human*, p. 391.
5. Michael J. Christensen, "With Liberty and Justice for All," *Herald of Holiness* 74, no. 23 (December 1, 1985): 7. Used by permission of publisher.

8

SOCIAL SERVICES FOR THE POOR

How to Manage Casework, Crisis Intervention, and Advocacy

Speak up for those who cannot speak for themselves, for the rights of all who are destitute. —Proverbs 31:8

"We are not social workers but carriers of Christ's love," says Mother Teresa about her two thousand Missionaries of Charity in seventy-seven countries.

The same is true for us who are involved in compassionate ministry. We are not simply social or mental health workers, we are urban missionaries and carriers of Christ's love. Our primary motivation is not money, social approval, or status, but the love of God and God's poor, which has its own reward. As Mother Teresa reminds us, "We do it for Jesus! It is his face we see in the faces of the poor."

Once our motivation and identity are clear, we can employ the best principles of social work, psychology, and medicine to do the work of Christ. Some urban churches and missions will be able to hire Christians who are trained and certified as professionals for support services. Others may have to rely totally on non-certified caseworkers and volunteers. Whether professional or not, paid or unpaid, we want to do Christ's work in the most responsible and professional way possible, bringing glory to God and healing to the individual who turns to us for help in time of need.

A commitment to support services requires basic knowledge and skills in the following disciplines: (1) casework, (2) crisis intervention, and (3) advocacy. The information in this chapter, while not diminishing the need for professionals on staff, provides general guidelines for the non-certified caseworker called to minister to mission contacts.

Casework Management

Once you decide to offer social services, counseling, and assistance with material needs, be prepared for a steady stream of "door people"—social service contacts who show up without an appointment. Dealing with unexpected people in need requires compassion, a thick skin, a cool head, and a systematic way to assess and address their needs. Casework, normally undertaken only by professionals, entails making decisions regarding availability, screening, assessment, referral, contracting, and empowerment.

Availability

The first consideration for the staff of a mission to consider is how often to be open for direct services. Needs can't all be met from 9:00 A.M. to 5:00 P.M., and unless you closely monitor the availability and resources of your staff and volunteers and train guests to come at certain times, your casework will not be of the quality that people deserve.

Post your hours of hospitality, support services, food and clothing distribution, and general operation. Then, be consistent. Don't promise more than you can deliver. Be clear about what you are offering and your limitations. Screen out those you cannot help, and do all you can for those with a potential for transition. Develop a reputation of responsible and compassionate service in your neighborhood.

The urban mission I direct is staffed by a mission director, a social worker, on-call counselors, intern assistants, and client volunteers. The social service office is open five days a week, 9:00 A.M.-12:00 M., for job counseling, casework, and spiritual direction.

In a neighborhood of 20,000 residents within a city of 750,000, we are in touch with over 1,000 poor and needy individuals representing a tenth of the city's homeless. It requires discipline to limit availability despite the overwhelming needs, but the longevity of ministry requires a more balanced life and reasonable schedule.

Screening

Each person who walks through the door is either a potential client or a time bandit. You must decide how to respond to the individual standing before you, based on previously set rules. Limiting the number of contacts you see each day is sound policy. There are also many reasons not to see a particular contact: You have limited time and resources; the individual may be unbearably demanding; the individual may be too drunk or high to respond rationally; the individual may not be telling you the truth. Careful screening is critical in avoiding case overload.

In order to screen a contact, you need to get some background information qualifying a person as a potential client. To maximize your impact in the city or the neighborhood, devote your energies first to those who are most needy and are appropriate for service.

Listen briefly to a person's story, then ask questions to confirm it. Ask for personal references who can verify the facts the client has offered, and be prepared to call them on the spot. If a potential client tells you he needs bus fare home, call his family and find out how they feel about it and whether they can reimburse the expense. If a woman says she needs money to help her child in the hospital, call the hospital to check out the story. Most stories are easily confirmed. Personally, I choose not to deal with people who do not level with me.

There are non-verbal ways to help screen contacts: Look for clues in body language, personal appearance, and physical mannerisms. Notice the person's countenance. Make eye contact and try to look deeply into the person's soul. Discern the spirit that this person exudes. Do you sense anxiety, hostility, or falseness? Is this person centered, peaceful, and trustworthy? After asking key questions, try to fill in the blanks with your intuition, and then go with your instincts.

When a mission contact is invited to become a service client, an appointment should be made with a caseworker to discuss his or her situation in privacy. Sometimes this can be done at the point of contact. More often, the particular person equipped to handle the case is not immediately available.

When an appointment is made, encourage the client to write the time down and to make every effort to be on time to meet with the caseworker. Following through with an appointment is a sign of sincere effort to advance. Failure to keep an appointment serves to further screen out those who are not seriously seeking help. Screening out con artists and contracting with those who can be helped can be accomplished through assessment of the needs that lie beyond the request for relief of an immediate problem.

Assessment

Suppose you are a staff member who has been assigned to help a client requesting shelter for the night. What are you to do?

156

Your first task in a private interview is assessment—determining the nature of the problem. Begin by establishing rapport with your client. Be genuinely interested, concerned, and helpful. The biggest complaint levied against government and institutional agencies is the impersonal treatment clients receive. Christian social workers and mission staff should exude the very spirit of Christ and treat every guest as a child of God.

After empathy and rapport are established, try to identify the real needs beneath the presenting problems. For example, an alcoholic may come to see you for a handout, but the real need may be encouragement to check into a detoxification program. A family may show up asking for money, but you might meet the need by offering groceries and directing them to the local public welfare office. A single mother may come to you for money when the real need is for disposable diapers for her baby. Someone who wants to hustle you for small change might be offered a short-term paying job. (It is best to avoid free handouts until a trusting client-to-caseworker relationship is established.)

The skill of assessment is in asking the right questions. Beneath presenting problems are underlying needs. It is the caseworker's job to assess the needs before exploring possible solutions. Start by finding out where this person came from and how he or she got to this point of need. Continue to probe, listening for clues, clarifying input, ascertaining behavior patterns, and discerning the spirit. When the mystery begins to make sense, make an initial assessment and decide what you can do to assist.

It is usually best to keep the assessment to yourself. Its value at this point is to help you determine the best course of action. Perhaps a referral should be made to another agency. Perhaps a second appointment should be recommended. Perhaps an ongoing client relationship is called for. Perhaps a simple word of encourage-

157

ment and support will send the person more successfully on his or her way. At the right time, in the right way, explore the options with your client and encourage him or her to choose a path that will lead to resolution and progress.

It is helpful, and sometimes policy, to record your session with a client on a profile sheet or file card. Such forms should include a person's name, address and phone number (if any), birthday, Social Security number, source of income, initial contact date, and other agencies visited. Every subsequent meeting with the client should be recorded, noting services rendered, tangible needs met, and general comments. Record-keeping not only serves a statistical purpose but supports a team approach to ministry. Others on staff need to know what has already been accomplished with a particular client so that they can proceed from there. Professionals keep records, and so should those who aspire to be.

Referral

An important aspect of casework is referral—supplying helpful information and making effective contacts for the client. Survival guides and social service resource directories are helpful for distribution, but letters of referral preceded by community networking are the caseworker's stock in trade.

A good caseworker will have fruitful relationships with key contacts in other social service agencies, which can be utilized on behalf of clients. If a battered woman comes to the mission center, for example, someone who knows who to call should be able to place her in a shelter or "safe house." If a homeless family needs a place to stay, a personal contact with shelter providers should be able to get them in.

Referral is relatively easy. You simply call the

appropriate service provider with whom you have previously networked (see chapter 4) and send the client over with a written form requesting assistance. Be sure to provide the client's name and any helpful comments.

All cities have specialized private social service agencies. These must be researched, compiled in a directory, and updated regularly to provide accurate information for successful referral. All cities have social service offices and federal programs providing Food Stamps, Supplemental Security Income (SSI), Aid to Families with Dependent Children (AFDC), General Relief or Assistance (GA), as well as Medicaid, Social Security, Medicare, children's nutritional programs, and senior meals. It is essential to understand these government programs and how to help clients obtain them. (See the Appendix for a summary of government subsidies and how to get food, money, and other benefits for your clients.)

Contracting

The purpose of screening is to select clients who can benefit from the service you provide. The purpose of assessment is to determine the nature of the problem. Referrals may solve immediate problems, but long-term casework is required to resolve deeper issues. This is where professionals are necessary and contracting important.

Contracting with a client establishes an accountability structure by which progress can be measured. Whether explicit or implicit, written or verbal, a contract specifies what both parties agree to do. The certified caseworker agrees to see the client regularly, arrange for needed services, and encourage the client along the way to recovery or transition. The client agrees to keep appointments, follow through with the

159

steps outlined in a session, and make an honest effort to advance.

A contract calls for realistic goals to be identified and agreed on. Goals then can be broken down into step-by-step objectives that the client can work toward one at a time. The certified caseworker helps the client commit to and fulfill the terms of the contract, personally, psychologically, physically, and vocationally.

As much as possible, clients themselves should actively make any necessary phone calls, follow through on assignments, explore options, and make choices. It is the certified caseworker's job to clarify matters, to encourage clients not to give up, and to hold them accountable for what they want to see happen in their lives within a mutually agreed-upon time frame. Commitment and accountability are essential for responsibility and success; without them one cannot advance.

Empowerment

The Reverend Jesse Jackson will be remembered at the Fourteenth Street Mission in Oakland for his empowerment sermon to the homeless: "When your back's against the wall, and you're trapped on every side . . . you gotta use what you got!" he shouted between illustrations.

To use what you got means to tap into your inner resources and connect with a power greater than yourself to do the otherwise impossible. A homeless man need not despair. A single mother need not give up. An alcoholic or co-dependent need not be defeated. Whatever the case, *when your back's against the wall, use what you got!*

An effective caseworker can remind clients who feel helpless of their own inner strengths and resources, as well as God's power to help. Together, client and caseworker can explore options, consider new possibilities, and tap into the Source from whom all blessings flow. The result will be *empowerment*—motivational strength and decisive action leading to advancement and successful accomplishment of goals.

Knocked Down But Not Crushed

Doris grew up in the Midwest. Her parents divorced when she was four, and although her mother did her best to raise her alone, Doris's childhood was physically and emotionally painful. At age six she was brought to live in a Christian children's home where she prayed to receive Christ.

Her life took on joy and stability when she went to live with her grandmother in Germany, but her grandmother died when Doris was just sixteen, and then she was on her own.

Doris studied in Europe and went on to earn an advanced degree in literature and linguistics. She returned to San Francisco in 1980 and worked as a teacher and as a door-to-door charity solicitor. But then, due to a series of difficult circumstances, her life "just fell apart."

On Christmas Day, Doris was unemployed, nearly broke, and making plans to leave her apartment because she couldn't pay rent or bills. She found herself alone on the beach, crying out to God for some sign of his love.

A few days after Christmas, she swallowed her pride and came to our neighborhood soup kitchen. There she saw a poster advertising hospitality and social services at the Oak Street House.

161

Doris came to the house during hospitality time. When she found an open door and a Christian welcome, she began to join us for Bible study. When we found out that Doris might soon be homeless, we set to work finding a new place for her to stay. We arranged for her to move into a Christian community center.

Today, the same woman who spent Christmas day alone, searching for a sign of God's love, is a happy and enthusiastic preschool teacher in a Christian school! Her transformation from loneliness and despair to rediscovering a Christ-centered life came through the provision of social services and the empowerment of Christian community.

Because people in need are hurting and often suspicious or reluctant to seek help, it is important to reach out first with simple gestures—like sharing a meal at a soup kitchen. Then they can be drawn further in with a warm hug and support services. And ultimately, some, like Doris, find themselves wrapped up in the loving embrace of Jesus, the power of God who strengthens us in our weakness.

Casework begins with availability, requires screening, assessment, referral, and contracting skills, and ends with empowerment from God to move ahead in strength and purpose. We turn now to a second aspect of social services—handling a crisis.

Crisis Intervention

Where do the poor and homeless turn in a moment of crisis? To the church or mission equipped to respond. Once your policies and procedures for routine visits are determined, go a step farther and plan how you will deal with emergencies. Responding to crisis situations involves (1) providing urgent medical attention, (2) suicide prevention, and (3) defusing assaultive clients.

Urgent Medical Attention

It is not unusual for regular clients to come to a mission center in a medical crisis even when a hospital emergency ward would be a more logical choice.

I will never forget the afternoon I was giving a tour of our mission facility to some out-of-town supporters. Suddenly, one of our homeless clients showed up at the front door in a panic. She had been stabbed on the bus and was bleeding. She needed to get to the hospital but was unwilling. It took our social worker, Ken Niles, a half hour of immediate attention and coaxing to get her to the emergency ward.

Suppose a person who has just been stabbed, beaten, raped, or otherwise hurt is brought to your mission center for help. What do you do first?

Assess the level of emergency and the intervention required. Should first aid be administered? Make sure someone on your staff has been trained in first aid and that everyone knows where the kit is kept. Should the police be called or an ambulance summoned? Are these numbers available and are these procedures clear to everyone working at the mission?

Next, try to prevent shock or panic by calm, directive leadership. Be prepared to have the person taken to the hospital or crisis care center. Most medical emergencies require swift and knowledgeable action, therefore basic training in crisis intervention is important.

Richard, whose tragic story is recounted in chapter 2, brought a traumatized woman to the Oak Street House. He confessed that he had been drinking and had raped this poor woman, and asked if we could help her. Our social worker, his head shaking in disbelief, enlisted my wife's support and summoned the police to get the woman to a crisis center. Richard was sorry and claimed he was out of control and in despair, and that no one loved him or could help him.

Suicide Prevention

Often in mission work you will get calls and visits from people in despair, contemplating suicide. Remember that all suicide threats must be taken seriously. Additionally, non-therapist counselors—including clergy, church counselors, and mission caseworkers—have a legal duty (at least in some states) to evaluate and refer suicidal persons to psychotherapists or psychiatric crisis centers, to ensure that they get there, and to warn family members of the danger![1]

How does one evaluate a suicide threat? Engage a depressed person in concerned conversation, asking pointblank questions regarding known risk factors. Substance abuse, chronic illness, and feelings of helplessness are the chief risk factors in suicide. Other factors to look for include inability to discuss the future meaningfully, loss of self-esteem, desire to be punished, fantasies about reunion with departed loved ones, hearing voices giving instructions about destroying oneself or others, and other signs of psychosis.

To determine the depth of the depression, ask questions such as the following: Have you felt hopeless or helpless in your situation? How do you feel about the future? Can you see yourself getting better? Do you blame yourself? Have you let friends or family down? Do you think much about death? Have you felt life is not worth living? Have you wished you were dead? Have you had thoughts about taking your life? Have you made any plans to do so?

Do not think it dangerous to ask counselees direct questions about suicide, as if you fear suggesting it to them. Experts say it is impossible to impose the thought of suicide. The invitation to talk openly about suicide may relieve a person's sense of isolation and hopelessness and assure him or her that you are not uncomfortable with the subject and may know how to help. Suicidal persons may not volunteer that they may soon kill themselves, but they will usually not deny it if asked.

Try to determine a person's "IPM"—intent, plan, and means—for carrying out a suicide threat. Is there a clear intent to harm oneself or others? Or is the person only moderately depressed and expressing needs that can be met? Has the person thought about a plan of suicide? Or is this an impulse that can be clearly defused? Has the person predetermined the means to carry out the plan? If so, there is a likelihood that an attempt will be made, if not now, then later.

Try to keep a dangerous person engaged in conversation or activity until good judgment returns to the despairing mind. Try to contract with the person not to hurt himself. Press for commitment: "Will you discuss this with me later this week?" "Will you come and see me tomorrow so we can talk this through?" "I'm coming over right now! Will you wait until I get there?"

Recognize the risk factors for suicide and aggressively intervene. Notify family members. Arrange for psychological consultation. Arrange for the suicidal individual not to be left alone. Suicide is preventable if love and concern are expressed, options explored, support given, and if the person commits to further dialogue.

I Just Called to Say . . .

Susie, whose four-year-old daughter died of a brain tumor and whose husband filed for divorce soon after,

165

was one of my counselees. I had been there for her when the baby was born and when she died. I saw her through two relationship breakups and received numerous phone calls "just to check in."

Sometimes Susie would snap into an uncontrollable rage and then gain composure. One night she called when she was on the streets alone and suicidal. She confessed her urge to "do something crazy" and allowed herself to be talked out of the threat.

Her mother and I discussed the matter, and I referred Susie to another counselor. She still calls me to "just to check in," and appreciates the fact that I cared enough to aggressively intervene.

Assaultive Clients

Any mission center open to street folks will attract some who are so angry they could explode in violence. This anger could be the direct result of feeling helplessly pushed around by other agencies before getting to yours. Or the anger could be the indirect result of years of damaged emotions and childhood traumas. The angry client may display a predictable temper spell or be unexpectedly hostile. The angry behavior may be a conscious attempt to gain needed services through intimidation, an unconscious psychotic break, or a result of drugs or alcohol.

Potentially assaultive people can be approached with confidence, kindness, and authority, which defuses their anger and allows them to be more reasonable and manageable. However, such a demeanor only can develop through experience. Sometimes symbols of authority and compassion help.

Have Collar, Will Travel

The reason I wear a clerical collar on city streets and in the mission center is for identity and protection.

Besides being a symbol of peace, authority, and holy purpose, a clerical collar can sometimes encourage an assaultive person to back away, as was the case one day in the seedy lobby of a San Francisco Tenderloin district hotel.

Stephen, a released mental patient and member of our church congregation, had gotten into a fistfight with a street alcoholic. Stephen had given his attacker two black eyes before the man pulled out a long, sharp corkscrew and threatened to knife him.

Stephen fled and recruited me to accompany him back to his room and to deal with the man. We confronted the angry man in the hallway, still staggering from intoxication and smarting from the fight.

"Stephen, you're a dead man!" he shouted.

"Hello, I'm Stephen's pastor," I managed to say, "and I think you two should agree not to fight anymore."

"I'm not religious," admitted the man, "and I'm going to kill Stephen!"

"When?" I asked.

"Right now is fine!"

"I think you better wait till tomorrow," I said as we prepared to leave.

The matter resolved itself the next morning. The drunk man had sobered up, apologized for his behavior, and promised to end the quarrel. He did not remember much about the incident, but he did remember the authority of the collar that caused him to back down.

How you will deal with a crisis must be thought through and rehearsed by your staff and volunteers prior to getting into a crisis situation. Here are some principles on dealing with assaultive clients employed by Golden Gate Ministries for staff training.

1. Engage the healthy part of the assaultive client's ego. Regardless of the cause of violent behavior, a rational and receptive part of the person's decision-making faculties is still intact. Speak to that part in a gentle but firm manner, directing the person to do what he or she needs to do. "You need to leave now!" or "Come with me outside and we'll discuss it" are helpful directions to repeat until followed.

2. Defuse the hostile atmosphere by isolating the client. Do not force a person out the door unless you are prepared for more violence or even a fight. Instead, ask the client to come with you and try to lead him or her outside or to an isolated area near the door. Another staff member should assist in the process. If the client refuses to be led and anger escalates, have someone call the police and ask all bystanders to leave.

3. Do not threaten or put the client in a win-lose situation. Speak with a low, calm, and steady voice; use short, pleasant, and positive words; don't crowd or violate personal space; lower your body to decrease the client's field of vision and to reduce client's fear of retaliation. Remember, you have the advantage for several reasons: The client's anger is not directed at you personally but at the "system"; you are calmer and more capable of clear thinking; you have backup available, both physically and psychologically; you are on home ground and the client is either a guest or an intruder.

4. Create a face-saving way out for the client that accomplishes the goal (averting violence) and preserves human dignity. Offer the person the opportunity to leave at any time; suggest alternatives, explore options. For example, say, "Seth, you need to leave now. Why don't you come back tomorrow. I'd like to talk to you about the situation privately, but this just isn't the right time or place." Be genuinely supportive of the client

while holding your ground. Remember that any client who has lost control is frightened and often relieved to have controls and parameters reestablished.

5. At the proper time and place, talk it out. A disruptive person will usually respond more positively if the fear of retribution is removed and the hope of being understood is conveyed. Start by asking, "What were your reasons for the outburst?" Keep the client on track by focusing on the primary problem. Once the threat of violence is diminished, behavior-related issues can be constructively explored. With a little creativity and common sense, volatile situations can be defused, and the peaceful environment of a compassionate mission center can be restored.

The third aspect of social services is the fine art of advocacy, which we will only briefly consider and illustrate.

Advocacy

In the Old Testament, to advocate means to

> Speak up for those who cannot speak for themselves,
>   for the rights of all who are destitute.
> Speak up and judge fairly;
>   defend the rights of the poor and needy.
> (Prov. 31:8-9)

In the New Testament, the Holy Spirit is our reference and guide. Jesus refers to the Spirit of God as the Paraclete or "Advocate," which literally means "to stand beside" in time of need (John 16:7). God's Spirit comes alongside us to comfort, empower, and advocate in our behalf (see also Rom. 8:26-27).

Members of the church of Jesus Christ, empowered by the Holy Spirit, are called to two levels of advocacy: client advocacy—to stand beside and speak up for the

169

powerless; and public policy advocacy—to stand up and speak up for kingdom principles and values in the face of unjust systems and oppression.

Client advocacy is necessary when a person is unable to adequately defend him or herself or is being denied justice because no one seems to care. A poor and needy family evicted from their tenement apartment may be too demoralized to fight; they may feel too insignificant for anyone to bother with. This family needs an advocate to defend their cause, stand up to the powers that be, and insist that their needs be met.

Client advocacy requires involvement, investment, and solidarity with people. Involvement means "sympathy with your sleeves rolled up above your elbow," as my urban ministry professor used to say. Investment means offering the time, energy, skill, and resources necessary to get things done. In the city, dealing with government bureaucracies, involvement, and investment are time-consuming. The result, however, is solidarity—standing with someone in time of need, adopting the needy person's cause as your cause, and making a commitment to become an advocate.

Public policy advocacy is necessary when you address the root causes of poverty and injustice. Sometimes we are called to confront the "principalities and powers" that war against God and keep the poor and oppressed unable to advance (Eph. 6:12). Social action, political lobbying, letter writing, phone calls, court appearances, demonstrations, and prophetic judgment are the basic tools of public policy advocacy.

Public policy advocacy can be illustrated by the difference between feeding the hungry and promoting kingdom values of simplicity of lifestyle and the sharing of resources. It is the difference between helping persons with AIDS and preventing the spread of the disease. It is the difference between treating the wounded in battle and stopping the makers of war. Both kinds of advocacy are needed, but prevention is better than treatment.

The story below, as told by social advocate Ron Sider, illustrates this distinction in the ministry of the church.

Ambulance Driver or Tunnel Builders?

A group of devout Christians once lived in a small village at the foot of a mountain. A winding, slippery road with hairpin curves and steep precipices without guard rails wound its way up one side of the mountain and down the other. There were frequent fatal accidents. Deeply saddened by the injured people who were pulled from the wrecked cars, the Christians in the village's three churches decided to act. They pooled their resources and purchased an ambulance. Over the years, they saved many lives although some victims remained crippled for life.

Then one day a visitor came to town. Puzzled, he asked why they did not close the road over the mountain and build a tunnel instead. Startled at first, the ambulance volunteers quickly pointed out that this approach (although technically quite possible) was not realistic or advisable. After all, the narrow mountain road had been there for a long time. Besides, the mayor would bitterly oppose the idea. (He owned a large restaurant and service station halfway up the mountain.)

The visitor was shocked that the mayor's economic interests mattered more to these Christians than the many human casualties. Somewhat hesitantly, he suggested that perhaps the churches ought to speak to the mayor. After all, he was an elder in the oldest church in town. Perhaps they could even elect a different mayor if he proved stubborn and unconcerned.

Now the Christians were shocked. With rising indignation and righteous conviction they informed the young radical that the church dare not become involved in politics. The church is called to preach the gospel and give a cup of cold water. Its mission is not to dabble in worldly things like social and political structures.

Perplexed and bitter, the visitor left. As he wandered out of the village, one question churned round and round in his muddled mind. Is it really more spiritual, he wondered, to operate the ambulances which pick up the bloody victims of destructive social structures than to try to change the structures themselves?[2]

Not all needs can be relieved or prevented. Not all social wrongs can be corrected in a lifetime, nor will all social service clients advance, make transitions, or find the health and wholeness they need. But individuals deserve the opportunity to honestly tell their story, have their basic needs met, feel empowered, and know that someone cares enough to stand with them against the spiritual principalities, political powers, and social structures that threaten to destroy human life. Christian social services, employing both professional and non-certified caseworkers engaging in support services and direct action, can achieve this purpose.

Notes

1. *Nally vs. Grace Community Church of the Valley,* Burbank, California—the first clergy malpractice case in the United States. The Court of Appeal created a new category of defendants called "non-therapist counselors," which includes pastors and church counselors as well as any other person who cannot prescribe drugs, is not licensed, and yet presents himself or herself as a counselor. According to the court, these non-therapist counselors have a legal duty to refer all individuals perceived to be suicidal to "those best able to prevent these counselees

from killing themselves." Additionally, non-therapist counselors have the legal duty to "insure that their counselees also are under the care of psychotherapists, psychiatric facilities, or others authorized and equipped to forestall an imminent suicide." There is also a duty to warn family members. Thus, a mere referral is not enough, in the court's judgment.

2. Ron Sider, *Ambulance Drivers or Tunnel Builders?* Tracts for Justice, published by Evangelicals for Social Action, P.O. Box 76560, Washington, D.C. 20013. Used by permission of publisher.

9

OPERATING A COMMUNITY HOUSE

Transition Through Residential Support

The Church must face the challenge of welcoming the homeless in Jesus' name, or being modern-day innkeepers with no room for Mary and Joseph who knock on our doors. —Dorothy Day

Earl was in the hospital suffering with the hepatitis he developed using dirty needles. When I visited him, he expressed his need to become a Christian. We prayed together, and I baptized him with a cup of water in his room. After being released, he was accepted into our community house program. He gave up drugs for three months, suffered a relapse, and was dismissed. Later, he got back on the path and slowly recovered from fifteen years of drug addiction.

Joshua was living in the park when he started coming to our community house for hospitality and social services. Substance abuse, mental illness, displacement, a broken family, personal chaos, and deliberate choice contributed to his homelessness. It was a definite risk to accept him into the residential program,

174

but we did. After two months of residency, he suffered an emotional setback and left the program unresolved.

Gregory, an alcoholic for twenty years, prayed to receive Christ at a mission Bible study. He was then invited to join the house community. After three months of tremendous progress, he chose to leave the program to recover on his own, a decision that turned out to be a spiritual setback.

Lyle met house community members at the Haight Ashbury Street Fair, and felt as if the Lord had directed his path. He had just come to faith in Christ and needed the support of Christian community. After growing up in an alcoholic family, feeling rejected and unloved, Lyle had been an alcoholic himself for twenty years. Now committed to sobriety and a new life, he applied to our residential program and was accepted.

Jim was suicidal, manic-depressive, and living in the fast lane in the gay community. He was reluctant to apply to the residential program that offered him the structure he needed to make the change he wanted deep inside. After considerable deliberation, Jim moved into the house and submitted to a process that would bring healing to his troubled spirit. He committed his life more fully to Christ, struggled with his sexual identity, and learned to lived with others. After three months of residency and Christian discipleship, Jim decided to try it on his own again and left town.

What these five men had in common was the opportunity to become mature Christians and advance in life through Christian discipleship and residential support at the Oak Street House—Golden Gate Ministries' "home for the homeless, refuge for the oppressed, and community for those called to urban ministry."

Why a Residential Program?

There are an estimated three million homeless people in the United States, and far more who have been adversely affected by displacement, unemployment, substance abuse, mental illness, and personal crisis.

Hospitality and social service programs can only relieve some of the symptoms of the problems people face on the streets. But a group home offering community support and accountability can assist people in transition from street survival to responsible living, from substance abuse to recovery, or from personal crises to emotional and spiritual stability.

A residential program that combines Christian discipleship, professional counseling, and the opportunity to learn life and work skills is an effective approach to empowering the underclass.

Jesus Christ, disguised as a homeless pilgrim, said, "I was a stranger and you invited me in" (Matt. 25:35). A group home provides a structure to welcome those Jesus called the "least of these." Dorothy Day, founder of the Catholic Workers Movement that established a national network of fifty community houses, suggested that every church and parish sponsor a house of hospitality. The church must face the challenge, she says, of welcoming the homeless in Jesus' name or being modern-day innkeepers with no room for Mary and Joseph who knock on our doors.

Golden Gate Ministries' Oak Street House is one urban model among many seeking to provide a stable, structured, and hospitable environment that fosters the essential components of a healthy Christian life: spiritual growth, personal responsibility, self-esteem, financial management, relationship skills, physical and emotional health, and employment development.

This chapter suggests ways that your church or

mission can start a community house at moderate expense. Once in operation, such a home can be sustained through program fees and church contributions. The guidelines that follow, developed over six years of trial and error, should save you time and effort in getting started.

Begin by identifying a population to be served and clarifying your program objectives. Then develop policies and procedures for operation, an employment program for rehabilitation, and a discipleship course for training. Finally, document and celebrate the transitions that take place in the life of the house ministry.

Who May Apply?

Community house ministries usually are intended for a specific population: single mothers, other women in need, men in transition, homeless families, troubled youth, released prisoners, recovering alcoholics, former drug abusers, or the physically or emotionally disabled.

The population selected will determine staffing needs and program design. Prayerfully choose a group of people your church or mission feels called to and equipped to serve. If single mothers are your target group, you will need staff members who have gone through the experience of single parenthood alone or who are specially trained in this particular area. If you wish to work with former prisoners, someone on staff needs to identify with their struggles. If you want recovering substance abusers in the program, find someone who has recovered and stabilized to run or be involved in the program. Similarly, a group home for the physically or emotionally disabled will require professional staffing and guidance.

Single men in transition are perhaps the easiest group to manage in a home, while single mothers as a group seem to have the highest motivation and potential for advancement. Any target group will have its unique set of problems and opportunities.

The Oak Street House program began by focusing on single men, ages eighteen to thirty-five, in transition, who had demonstrated through their attitudes and behavior a commitment to personal, emotional, vocational, and spiritual growth and who were willing to work out a plan for stabilizing their lives and achieving their goals. (Such a plan of action was worked out with a staff counselor and monitored weekly.)

Situations that made an applicant eligible for the program included homelessness; eviction or displacement; a personal crisis requiring intervention; a recent release from jail or prison; a recovery still in progress from drug or alcohol abuse; dependence on the public welfare system; negative, destructive, or unhealthy environments; or referral by other churches or agencies for special need.

Individuals who did not qualify for program admittance included current substance abusers, individuals with medical or psychological difficulties requiring long-term medication or therapy, mental patients, individuals who demonstrated a chronic pattern of self-destructive behavior, and individuals unwilling to commit themselves to life change and personal growth.

Clarifying Program Objectives

The needs of each potential population group are critical and manifold. It is important to identify in writing what it is that we can do, given our facilities, staffing, and resources. Begin by addressing basic physical needs, include medical and psychological needs that can reasonably be addressed, and do not neglect the needs of the spirit.

For example, the Oak Street House had these program objectives: *(a)* to provide short-term housing to six men per night; *(b)* to provide three nutritious meals per day to residents; *(c)* to provide clothing and personal hygiene supplies; *(d)* to supervise residents and support them in their plans of action; *(e)* to provide individual counseling; *(f)* to provide pastoral and community support, sponsorship, and accountability; *(g)* to arrange for medical and psychological services as needed; *(h)* to assist with educational opportunities as required; *(i)* to provide spiritual direction and Christian discipleship; *(j)* to assist with vocational training, job search, and employment development.

These ten initial objectives proved to be more than our staff could deliver. After a year we had to close the program, reevaluate our target group and objectives, and reopen with more manageable objectives.

Once your target group is identified and the program objectives are clear, you need an interdisciplinary team to manage the program. Most community houses of six to twelve residents will minimally require a house manager and an assistant, one of whom will need to live on the premises. These two staff members may be supported by professional counselors, social workers, and resource persons on an "as needed" basis. A pastor or chaplain can be called upon from the church community to provide spiritual direction and discipleship training. Volunteers can be recruited for group activities and employment development. Such a team stands a good chance of making a difference in the lives of the residents.

Developing Policies and Procedures

As part of your interdisciplinary team, it is best to hire a social service professional to develop a policies and procedures manual based upon the goals of the ministry and the objectives of the program for the group home you envision. Such a document should include procedures for program admittance, policies and procedures for daily maintenance, program offerings, accountability measures and methods of disciplinary action, and termination procedures. The following policies and procedures were developed by Carmen Berry for the Oak Street House:

a. Program admittance: The first step in applying to the program is reading a program description and filling out a questionnaire. The application form for the Oak Street House program includes questions about the applicant's life experience, family contacts, educational and religious background, personal goals, and personal references.

When an application is turned in, a screening interview is scheduled with the house manager, during which the following questions are discussed:

- What are your reasons for applying? (presenting problem)
- How did you learn about the program? (referral source)
- How would you prioritize your goals? What is your plan for advancing? (commitment level)
- What is your source of income, and how will you pay the program fees? (financial status)
- Are you facing any medical, legal, or family difficulties? (personal issues)
- What is your experience with alcohol and drugs? (substance abuse history)

A residential committee reviews the applications, is informed about the screening interview, and determines who should be admitted. Qualified candidates may be asked to take a personality test and meet with a counselor for psychological assessment. If a candidate has been denied admittance, the house manager explains this decision, provides support for the candidate if such a decision is a major disappointment, and assists in locating a more appropriate program. If someone just needs a place for the night, a judgment call is made and a guest room possibly offered.

A candidate who is accepted into the program is either put on a waiting list or, if space allows, is scheduled to move in. An intake interview occurs in which the candidate's questions are answered, expectations discussed, goals and objectives clarified, and a residential contract drawn up.

The residential contract outlines the resident's daily schedule, housekeeping assignments, agreement to obey rules and pay program fees, and commitment to work on the plan of action. The plan of action includes how progress will be measured in four goal areas: spiritual life, employment/education, mental health, and personal development. The contract is valid for three months at a time and is then renegotiable. Contract violation is grounds for disciplinary action or immediate dismissal.

A minimum of a $300 per month program fee and volunteer work in the mission is required of each resident. Residents with less ability to pay are encouraged to increase their income through General Assistance (welfare), Food Stamps, or work credits. No candidate is disqualified for inability to pay the program fee.

b. Policies and procedures: The house manager is responsible for establishing a reasonable time for getting up each morning, leading the community in a daily devotional and time of prayer, and monitoring a daily routine.

Those wanting breakfast are to be at the table, showered and dressed for the day, at a specific time. Each resident is responsible for preparing his own lunch. The evening meal is prepared on a rotating basis

181

at a regularly scheduled time. Community meals provide opportunities for the house manager to promote support and participation among residents, encourage sharing of struggles and victories, and to better assess the progress of each resident.

The kitchen is to be cleaned following each meal. Rooms are to be cleaned daily and chores accomplished weekly. The house manager is responsible for inspecting and enforcing cleanliness in the house. Curfew at 11:00 P.M. is important, though difficult to enforce.

House rules apply at all times and must be enforced to ensure community stability. Oak Street House residents are expected to be productive during the day (job, school, or volunteer work) and to attend community activities (worship services, Bible studies, and group meetings). Residents are responsible for anyone they allow in the house. No overnight guests are permitted without permission and clearance. Phone calls may be made from a pay phone, or if a community phone is available, calls must be recorded. House keys are provided to residents with a proven record of responsibility and progress. Nothing may be brought into the house that would disturb the spiritual atmosphere that is sought: no weapons, drugs, alcohol, tobacco, fighting, abusive language, disruptive behavior, dishonesty, or stealing.

c. Program offerings: What must be avoided in any community house are idleness and low morale. You avoid them by providing a full program of weekly activities, including Bible studies and worship services, discipleship training sessions, work and activity times, and community meetings in which are discussed housekeeping issues, meal planning, and personal concerns.

What must be fostered is a sense of community—that each resident has equal worth and responsibility in the house, that role distinctions exist and have a purpose in the body of Christ, but that our identity is one in the

Lord. Toward this end, Golden Gate Ministries also sponsors an annual retreat and a wilderness expedition during which participants learn about their unique gifts and build trust as a community of faith.

d. Accountability and disciplinary action: At the end of each day, the house manager reviews the activity of each resident, noting progress and areas of concern. Positive reinforcement in the form of privileges are offered in moments of progress and negative reinforcements in the form of reprimands and demerits are given out for any violations of policies, schedule, rules, or personal contract.

Every week the staff reviews each resident's progress or lack thereof. Three demerits results in a counseling session with the residential committee. Five demerits results in probation and loss of key privileges. Any resident acquiring six demerits is subject to dismissal. Demerits can disappear with time and progress.

After the first month and at the end of each three month contract period thereafter, an evaluation of social living skills and contract compliance takes place between the staff and the resident.

The Oak Street House evaluation form measures progress in the following areas: personal discipline, employment/education, financial management, health and fitness, spiritual life, relations with other mission residents, and relations with staff. A favorable evaluation results in greater privileges and a renewed contract. An unfavorable evaluation has no reward.

e. Termination: A residential program is completed when, in the course of nine months to a year, a resident has made significant progress toward realizing personal, emotional, spiritual, and vocational goals and is able to make a transition.

When a resident is ready to graduate from the program, much attention should be called to the event. A certificate of completion should be presented, public recognition arranged, and a special meal or party planned. For many graduates, it will be the major accomplishment of their lives.

Finally, a closure should take place. This is a time when the graduate's records are reviewed and progress is celebrated. The entire period of residency should be rehearsed, noting high points and low points along the way. Friendly advice can be given for what lies ahead.

If assistance in locating housing is needed, it should be offered during the final two weeks of residency. If program fees are still owed, arrangements for payments should be made. An affirmative hug and an invitation to stay involved as an alumnus of the house community will serve to encourage the graduating resident to keep in touch. The staff should make every effort to track the progress of residents after they leave the program.

Employment Development

An effective community house ministry will include an employment development program of some kind. Getting a job and having a vocation do not come as easily to the homeless as those who are securely employed imagine. Sometimes unemployment is the result of poor choices, sometimes the job market is to blame, but most often it is the result of a lack of work skills for the modern economy.

There are at least three ways to incorporate job development into your community house ministry. Begin by simply posting work opportunities on a bulletin board and encouraging residents to apply. This may evolve into a mission employment agency placing applicants in appropriate jobs. Sometimes grants are available for vocational rehabilitation—creating jobs or training programs with graduated stress levels leading toward the goal of participants earning their way in the world. Ministry-sponsored business ventures that create jobs and can become income producing for the ministry are an even better way to go, as Golden Gate Ministries is discovering.

A mission employment agency requires a steady stream of willing and able workers and compassionate contacts in industry. Most urban churches, rescue missions, and social service organizations are in touch with hard-to-employ persons who could qualify (if someone would work to connect them) for entry level, unskilled, and semiskilled job opportunities. When such a program is successful, both workers and employers will continue to seek out the agency to meet their labor needs.[1] While such a program assists willing workers, it does not address the needs of the unmotivated or of those who need a rehabilitative bridge to the work world.

Vocational rehabilitation requires subsidy and networking to create jobs and provide training for those who are deficient in work skills. The state employment security office offers programs to help people learn skills, determine vocational aptitude, and find jobs, as well as paying disability and unemployment benefits. Urban missions can teach the unemployed why people get jobs and keep them, and such practical skills as resume preparation, acting on job opportunities, facing the interview, and persistence and follow-through.

Golden Gate Ministries, with an initial $20,000 grant from Nazarene Compassionate Ministries, began a Employment Development Program to train and employ selected residents and social service clients in San Francisco. Its stated purpose was to "provide a bridge for those wanting to make a leap from being dependent on society or dropouts from it, to being independent and autonomous within it."[2] We desired to create opportunities for the willing but not-yet-able workers to be productive through the provision of supervised work experience, community service, and creative output.

The program was designed by Michael Mata to function as follows: The work pace and demand is

185

patterned to the working habits each participant brings into the program. Over time, the demands of work projects are increased as participants work through their dysfunctional habits. This process, called "graduated stress," is implemented in a variety of ways: by increasing productivity demands, by attendance and punctuality requirements, by assigning workers to increasingly complex work projects, by gradually decreasing the intensity of supervision, and, when necessary, by demoting or releasing from the program participants who are not making progress.[3]

Participants in the program begin working with low skill, low intensity in-house projects, progress to labor-intensive outstationed work projects, and graduate into income-generating work opportunities. Along the way, the ministry provides support services such as job counseling, work skill training, and personal encouragement.

In-house projects are created in the community house and immediate neighborhood. Participants are hired at minimum wage to do housecleaning, building maintenance, clothing room organization, and other odd jobs. Neighborhood projects might include volunteering at the soup kitchen, family shelter, or community garden, or cleaning up the streets. Social service clients are paid a "gratuity" and house residents can earn "work credits" that apply to their program fees.

Outstationed work projects are managed by host companies directly compensating either the ministry (for the benefit of the participants) or the workers (at an agreed-upon wage). Work projects might include general maintenance, construction, landscaping, painting, moving, or sales. The ministry receives a portion of each worker's compensation to cover screening, administration, and transportation costs. The host company is freed of the need to recruit, and in some cases, to supervise the work crew. And the ministry is freed of overhead and project management. An employment supervisor is required to recruit workers, supervise the labor force, and generate work projects.

Business ventures, a third-phase option, are income-generating enterprises managed by a ministry, employing selected residents and clients who have progressed from in-house activities and outstationed projects and who are ready for the completion of the rehabilitative process. Work experience in a ministry venture should serve to assess and test a participant's capacity to function in the mainstream employment world and bridge the gap.

Non-profit business ventures generally are either product oriented (like woodworking, toy manufacturing, brush assembly) or service oriented (like janitorial work, painting, construction subcontracting). Consult with a business person in your church or on your board as to all the necessary requirements for starting and running a business, and make sure it is directly related to your organization's mission purpose (i.e., rehabilitative employment). Otherwise, your venture will be taxed as a for-profit business.

Golden Gate Ministries created in-house work projects, outstationed projects, and a business venture with moderate success. Drawing from a resource bank of a thousand social service clients, not more than twenty-five at any one time became part of the work force. In a year's time, over fifty clients received supervised work experience through the job development program.

In-house work projects included housecleaning, sorting clothing for distribution, maintenance, and repair. Out-stationed projects have included building maintenance and renovation, painting, moving, construction, demolition, janitorial services, carpet cleaning, landscaping, bulk mailing, product sales, furniture refinishing, and clerical services.

We tried unsuccessfully to start a health food store in the neighborhood, and explored the feasibility of a toy

187

manufacturing venture as well as print shop. Under the entrepreneurial leadership of mission director Mike Davis, we settled on a business servicing general contractors and home owners who need our work crew for cleaning, carpentry, painting, and repair. Three or four workers at a time are assigned to a project, and both the ministry and the laborers benefit from the business.

Work and industry are healthy activities. They instill hope and dignity and are an essential part of Christian discipleship.

Discipleship Training

The primary purpose of a Christian community house is not simply to provide shelter and structure for people in transition but to offer spiritual direction and discipleship training to residents who want to mature in faith. This can be accomplished one-on-one as well as by a weekly group discipleship session.

Designate at least one evening a week for a common meal followed by Christian teaching and discussion. I favor a yearlong series covering four major areas of study: spiritual formation, stewardship, gifts for ministry, and life skills.

a. Spiritual formation includes practical instruction in how to pray, how to read and study the Scriptures, and the importance of meditation. The emphasis of this first phase of discipleship is on spiritual grounding (being connected to the source of life in a personal relationship with God) and character development (allowing the Scriptures to inform our faith and practice).

b. Stewardship of time, talent, and treasure is a three-month mini-course on divine ownership and human management of what has been entrusted to our care. Time management is taught from the perspective that God desires that we make the best of every opportunity (Eph. 5:15-16). Discovering and investing our talents is taught from the perspective that God holds us accountable for developing the natural gifts and abilities hidden in our hearts (Matt. 25:14-30). Responsible use of our earthly treasure (material resources) is taught with the following principles in mind: detachment (Luke 12:22-34), contentment (Phil. 4:12-13), simplicity (Luke 12:13-34), and generosity (Prov. 11:25).

c. *Gifts for ministry* is a three-month mini-course on the body of Christ and how God has distributed resources and talents to each unique member of the family for the common good. After identifying at least fourteen spiritual gifts in Scripture and how they function in the life of the body, the discipleship group completes a questionnaire designed to reveal what gifts each one seems to possess. By considering the confirmations of others, we try to identify our particular ministry.

d. *Life skills* are principles that many take for granted but that are essential for successful living in the world. The following list of basic skills, though not exhaustive, is enough to occupy three months of special emphasis: self-disclosure (why am I afraid to tell you who I am?), suppressing impulses (I don't always have to do what I want!), delaying gratification (sacrifice now with a reward later), relinquishing (let go and let God), the art of listening (I hear you), confronting (mirror back what you see), resolving conflict (make "I" statements), being straightforward (be clear with people), persisting (finish what you start), goal setting (know what you want), positive thinking (how's my PMA—positive mental attitude?), being resourceful (use what you've got), breaking patterns (know your historical weaknesses), having confidence (know who you are in God), being intentional (know what you're doing), taking initiative (put it out there), and committing to action(take the risk).

189

After each quarter of discipleship training, a "take-home" exam is given as a further teaching tool. At the end of the year, residents are better equipped to face what life demands and God requires. Graduation occurs, and transitions can be celebrated when Christian discipleship is effective.

Celebrating Transitions

A community house ministry should be committed to documenting people's stories and struggles and to communicating to others the ways God works in lives. Everyone has a unique story that deserves to be told, even if it's just a slice of one's life.

Tracking Three Residents

1. Carlos was one of our mission residents who did not find success in the Oak Street House program. He had been a San Francisco jazz musician before alcoholism destroyed his livelihood. After three attempts at sustaining a marriage, an unsuccessful military career, and dealing with his sister's suicide, Carlos proceeded to drink himself to death.

On his deathbed, the only friend or family member the doctors could contact was Lori Follin-Dotson, associate pastor of Golden Gate Community, whose card was in his pocket. For weeks she had accompanied him to AA meetings. Church members had befriended him. The mission had taken him in. But ultimately, Carlos had to take responsibility for his own life. His death caused us all to realize that God calls us not to success but to obedience. It is for God to determine the results of our faithfulness.

2. *James was one of our residents who graduated after a year in the community house. James remembers growing up unsettled and unhappy. "I really had no friends and only a brief interaction with my three older siblings." His junior high and high school years were equally depressing, he recalls.*

After years of trying to find his path, he heard about the Oak Street House and applied to the residential program. "I viewed my acceptance as a culmination of my spiritual journey that began in high school."

It was the program's purpose to support James and the other residents in their spiritual, emotional, personal, and vocational development. We assist people in transition from basic survival to responsible living and working in the world through Christian discipleship.

In the year that James was with us, he worked both in the house for work credits and outside the house for pay. He also completed a ten-month training program at John Adams Community College as a medical assistant—his first real accomplishment. He now has two professional certificates—geriatric home aide and medical transcribing.

Several of us were present at his graduation ceremony and heard the touching speech he gave: "It's been a really tough program. There were times when I wanted to give up. The tests and teachers were demanding. But I made it through. I want to thank my parents for supporting me, and my community at the Oak Street House. Most of all, I want to thank God. I believe in a Power greater than myself without whom I wouldn't have made it. Thank you very much!"

After graduation James pounded the pavement and landed a full-time job as a geriatric home aide. He left the program and moved into an apartment in the neighborhood. As an alumnus, he is welcome at the house and is invited to participate in the mission activities.

3. David, through raised a Nazarene in Idaho, was a fugitive from the law and living in the park when he knocked on the door of the Oak Street House to get a blanket. When he found out the mission was sponsored by the church of his youth, he was surprised and became a frequent guest for coffee.

He eventually was extended residency status and became part of the house Bible study group. He recommitted his life to Christ and asked for prayer from his friends. Letters were written in his behalf, and David was cleared of his legal charge.

During his nine months of residency, David made his transition from street survival to employment in the city. He worked initially in the job development program and later as a hotel desk clerk and ship's cook. After three years of transitional employment, David landed a secure job in a prestigious publishing firm in San Francisco.

David defines home as "somewhere to come back to." After years of roaming, setbacks, and successes, Christian community became the home he never had. For him, a residential program was a key to spiritual stability and responsible living in the world.

Success cannot be measured in one standard way. Each case falls into a category. The Oak Street House is most effective in crisis intervention cases (i.e., with people who are homeless due to tragic circumstances, personal chaos, or legal problems). We are least effective with chronic cases like substance abusers and the mentally ill.

Statistically, about a fourth of those who are accepted into the program make a successful transition to sustaining a job, maintaining an apartment, and growing in spirit. Half the residents suffer setbacks along the way, and the remaining portion seem unaffected by the program. Is a 25 percent "success rate" cost-justified and spiritually significant? Jesus Christ himself predicted no higher results when he told the parable of the Sower:

> "Listen! A farmer went out to sow his seed. As he was scattering the seed, some fell along the path, and the birds came and ate it up. Some fell on rocky places, where it did not have much soil. It sprang up quickly, because the soil was shallow. But when the sun came up, the plants were scorched, and they withered because they had no root. Other seed fell among thorns, which grew up and choked the plants, so that they did not bear grain. Still other seed fell on good soil. It came up, grew and produced a crop, multiplying thirty, sixty, or even a hundred times." Then Jesus said, "He who has ears to hear, let him hear." (Mark 4:3-9)

A community house ministry should expect to sow a lot of seed, realizing that 25 percent will be devoured by birds, 25 percent will not take root, 25 percent will not bear grain, and 25 percent will yield a good crop. If we measure our ministry by the harvest alone, we will be discouraged. If we measure our ministry by the faithfulness it takes to continue sowing seeds of love and opportunity, we can leave the results in God's hands.

Summary

The ideal picture of a Christian community house ministry looks something like this: A homeless person knocks on the door in need of food, clothing, or shelter. Hospitality is extended in Jesus' name. An appointment is made to see a caseworker. Clothing and hygiene supplies are offered. Food services and housing are arranged. The guest is invited to stay for a Bible study or

193

a worship service. He continues to attend weekly meetings and seeks spiritual direction and counseling.

After some time has passed, the staff invites him to apply to the residency program. He goes through the process and is accepted. Community life proves to be a supportive and healing environment. The staff works with him in a discipleship program that includes spiritual direction, stewardship, life skills, work skills, and counseling. He begins to look for a job and think about a vocation. He joins the work force and begins to earn his way. He has left the old life behind. He has made a new commitment to Christ. He is ready for church and a ministry of his own, for he has taken advantage of every opportunity the group home has to offer. In nine months to a year, he will be ready for independent Christian living and working in the mainstream.

Although an urban mission will offer social services to thousands each year with basic and special needs, community house ministries are content to invest quality time and effort in just a few, knowing that some, like Carlos, will not make it, but hoping that those like James and David will make their transition.

Notes

1. Jubilee Jobs, a ministry of The Church of the Savior in Washington, D.C., is an outstanding model of a mission employment agency.
2. From the Golden Gate Ministries manual, "Rehabilitative Employment Program," designed by Michael Mata, 1986.
3. Ibid.

10

AIDS—THE NEW LEPROSY
How to Start an AIDS Ministry

By the end of 1991, an estimated 270,000 cases of AIDS will have occurred. . . . It is the responsibility of every citizen to be informed about AIDS and to exercise the appropriate preventative measures. —C. Everett Koop, M.D.
United States Surgeon General

Historically, people have been forced to cope with plagues and deadly disease. In every case, opportunities to respond with fear or courage were present.

Leprosy, from early accounts in the Bible to modern times, has been a feared contagious disease. Lepers were ostracized by society, quarantined as "unclean"—both physically and spiritually—and excluded from the community. No one dared touch a leper for fear that the sinful disease would be caught.

In the sixteenth century, the bubonic plague wiped out one-third of Europe's population. In London, according to historical records, most physicians fled their practices and many clergy deserted their pulpits. Seventy thousand of the 400,000 citizens died. People lost faith in both the medical profession and the institutional church.

In the 1830s, when cholera was rampant in America, the rich blamed the poor and burned their humble dwellings to stop the spread of the disease.

During the early 1900s, tuberculosis was the crippling disease. Many who got it were committed to sanatoriums against their will.

Between 1918 and 1920, influenza killed over 500,000 people in America, causing fear and hysteria throughout the world.

Now, at the close of the twentieth century, the AIDS epidemic is gripping the world with fear. Once again, there is a tendency to assign blame and persecute the victim. Will panic prevail, or will education and compassion cast out fear? Much depends on how the church responds.

This chapter reviews the facts and addresses the issues of the AIDS epidemic. It also celebrates how some churches are responding to the crisis and suggests ways a group might start an AIDS ministry.

The AIDS Epidemic

Both credible and incredible speculations about the origins of AIDS continue to be advanced. Although no one knows how the AIDS virus developed, we do know how it spreads and the effect it has on its victims. There is no cure, there is a degree of risk, and there is a need for compassionate ministry.

What are the medical facts about AIDS, and how are we to assess the risks of ministry?

Acquired Immune Deficiency Syndrome (AIDS) is activated when human immunodeficiency virus (HIV) gets into the bloodstream through sexual contact or injection and causes a breakdown in the body's normal defenses against infection and disease. AIDS leaves one vulnerable to "opportunistic diseases" such as Kaposi's sarcoma (KS), *Pneumocystis carinii* pneumonia (PCP), and numerous other diseases not usually fatal in people with normal immune systems.

AIDS is an elusive and deadly virus requiring a blood host. When no host is present, it dies in forty to fifty seconds. The virus is quite susceptible to a variety of disinfectants, including household bleach.

AIDS is a contagious disease, but it is difficult to catch. Medical researchers who have studied every case of AIDS since the epidemic began have concluded that there are only three ways the disease is transmitted in the United States: (1) through blood contamination, (2) through intimate sexual contact, and (3) through an infected mother to her unborn baby.[1] Infected blood, when passed from one person's body fluids to another's—orally, anally, genitally, or directly through injections and transfusions—dramatically increases the risk of contracting the AIDS virus.

Despite popular concerns and reports that the AIDS virus has been found in tears and saliva, there is no evidence to support theories that AIDS can be transmitted through tears, saliva, urine, eating utensils, vaccines, insects, or casual contact.[2]

The incubation period for AIDS varies from a few months to several years before symptoms appear. A person can be an AIDS virus carrier (HIV positive) without developing the disease. When a person contracts AIDS, the following symptoms may appear: extreme fatigue; fevers, chills or night sweats; rapid weight loss for no apparent reason; swollen lymph glands; white spots or unusual blemishes in the mouth; persistent or dry cough; diarrhea; and blotches or bumps on the skin.

According to the United States Surgeon General, C. Everett Koop, no medical cure for AIDS is expected in this century. However, researchers worldwide are searching for a vaccine to prevent its spread and for a way to treat the disease. Several drugs, especially AZT, are being tested and are available to arrest some of the effects of AIDS.

The World Health Organization refers to AIDS as an epidemic of global proportions. Countries from every continent are reporting cases, with particularly high

197

rates of incidence in Central Africa, North America, Europe, and Latin America. Since its advent, over ten million people worldwide have been infected with AIDS. At least 200,000 have actually contracted the disease.[3]

Although the disease may have been introduced to America as early as the mid 1960s, the first reported case of AIDS was in 1981. Today, between 1.5 and 3 million people in America have been infected, 48 percent of whom are expected to develop the disease within six years. Another 100,000 to 300,000 people in America are expected to come down with AIDS Related Complex (ARC)—a technically milder form of immune deficiency disease which usually develops into full-blown AIDS sometime later. At the time of this writing, 54,723 cases of AIDS have been reported to the Centers for Disease Control since 1981, and 30,715 of these people have died.[4] The disease has doubled and may continue to double every eighteen months until the end of the twentieth century, when, according to the Surgeon General, as many as 100 million worldwide may die from AIDS.[5]

Although the Centers for Disease Control projections change daily, it is staggering to consider the grim forecast; 270,000 cumulative cases of AIDS in 1991; 54,000 deaths from AIDS in 1991 alone![6]

The AIDS epidemic represents an extraordinary time in human history, and calls for extraordinary intervention. What has hindered a swift and compassionate response from society and the church are the moral implications of AIDS.[7]

Is AIDS a Punishment from God?

How can we interpret the reality that AIDS frequently affects those whose lifestyle puts them at high risk?

In the United States, seven years after the disease was identified, at least 73 percent of AIDS cases are in the gay community. Those in the gay community who have anal intercourse with multiple sexual partners are at the highest risk of exposure to the virus. Users of intravenous drugs make up 25 percent of the cases. Those who reuse dirty syringes and needles face the highest risk. The remaining 2 percent of AIDS cases affect hemophiliacs, recipients of blood transfusions, children born to infected mothers, and heterosexual partners of AIDS carriers.[8]

Is it possible that AIDS is a "plague sent by God" to punish or convince gays and addicts to change their ways? How specific and targeted is God's judgment in this lifetime? Are Christians to rejoice and participate in God's judgment? Such questions require both theological reflection and simple logic.

It is true that AIDS hit the American gay community the hardest. However, in Africa the heterosexual population is most severely infected. Half of these are women. Are we to conclude from this that God is punishing American gays and African couples? Or are we to conclude that only the "sexually immoral" get AIDS? If AIDS is God's judgment on immoral lifestyles, why is God so selective about who gets punished?

AIDS is affecting the black and Hispanic populations in America at twice the expected rate. (Eighteen percent of the population of the United States is black or Hispanic, yet these groups account for 41 percent of the nation's AIDS cases.) Is God punishing blacks and Hispanics more than whites? Again, if immorality brings God's judgment in the form of AIDS, is immorality more prevalent in minority communities than in the white majority?

Children are now dying of AIDS in increasing numbers. One out of sixty-one babies born in New York City in 1987 tested positive for the AIDS virus, and unborn babies are contracting the disease in their mothers' wombs. By 1991, medical professionals expect at least five thousand cases of children with AIDS. If AIDS is a direct consequence of sin, then why do the innocent suffer? Does God punish children for the sins of their parents?

Lesbians are assumed by the uninformed to be a high-risk group, simply because they are homosexual. Yet sexual relations between lesbians account for zero percentage of AIDS cases. Are we to conclude that lesbians are protected from the plague? In the words of one social satirist, "If AIDS is God's judgment on gay men, then lesbians must be God's chosen people!"

The judgment theory raises more moral questions than it answers. The facts show that AIDS is no respecter of persons. It spreads in specific ways regardless of the sexual orientation or spiritual condition of the transmitter or receiver. Avoiding certain sexual activities (such as anal intercourse), taking precautions (such as using condoms), limiting oneself to one sexual partner (as in marriage), avoiding intravenous drug use, and the screening of blood donations will reduce the risk of AIDS, but the disease can potentially infect anyone.

The problem with "plague theology"—attributing sickness and disease directly to God's intention to punish—is that it gives false justification for God's people not to get passionately involved with those who suffer. As one Christian layperson asked me upon finding out our Christian community was involved in AIDS ministry: "Why are you trying to interfere with what God is doing in the world?"

In one sense, all sickness and disease exists because of sin and careless neglect. Actions have consequences that we can interpret as God trying to tell us something. Smoking, for example, has been medically linked to lung cancer. People aware of this may feel God wants them to give up cigarettes. But only a theology that attributes evil to God asserts that God specifically punishes cigarette smokers with cancer. AIDS is a disease, as is cancer and the common cold. There are natural outcomes, not divine afflictions, from exposure to germs and viruses. Any other theology negates the revelation of God's compassionate nature.

Jesus confronted the theology of his day that viewed physical affliction as punishment for sin: " 'Rabbi, who sinned, this man or his parents, that he was born blind?' 'Neither this man nor his parents sinned,' said Jesus, 'but this happened so that the work of God might be displayed in his life' " (John 9:2-3).

Could it be that AIDS, rather than being viewed as "punishment" from God for sin, is in some way a "word" from God—a call to his people to respond with compassion to those who might otherwise die without knowing they are loved? The question remains: Will the church respond with hysteria and judgment, or with wisdom and compassion?

The Church Responds: Ministry in Time of Plague

Both mainline and evangelical churches, though slow to respond, have begun embracing persons with AIDS. Across the nation and the world, especially in major cities with high incidence rates, church communities are committing resources, and mission groups are organizing to minister compassionately to those affected by the new plague.

Persistent voices in my own church and mission sounded the call to do something in response to the AIDS epidemic in San Francisco. Ambitious plans were proposed, a handful of persons with AIDS were responded to with compassion, but no programmatic commitments were made. Finally, a few weeks before Easter 1987, six years after the crisis began, a group of us attended an interfaith symposium on AIDS ministries

201

in San Francisco with the intention of becoming more active in our response.

One of the conference conveners gave an impassioned presentation on the need for the church to be the church and reach out with God's love to people. What pierced my heart were these words: "The gay community seeking to care for their own responded first to the AIDS crisis. For this they deserve our highest affirmation. The medical community and mental health workers showed up second to the crisis. The doctors, nurses, social workers, and other professionals who cared enough to respond to what society called a 'gay disease' deserve our next highest honor. Finally, the church arrived on the scene. Thank you for coming! Realize you're late, but we're glad you're here!"

After the gentle scolding was over, I raised my hand to say, "I'm a minister in the Church of the Nazarene, and there are four others from my church here with me. We realize we are late, but we're here and we want to help. What can we do?"

Motivated by the possibilities for ministry, we formed an AIDS mission group to determine what to do. Ten of us gathered on the first Saturday morning after Easter and committed ourselves to meet weekly in prayer and discussion as a support group. Our agenda: to discern what God was calling us to do as individuals and as a community to serve, as Jesus did, the outcasts of society.

We began by learning what other churches in our city had been doing in AIDS ministry. The director of the AIDS Interfaith Network met with us and recounted how he and a small group had prayed weekly for a year on the steps of the Roman Catholic cathedral. The official church response was a weekend of prayer and a special mass for persons with AIDS.

Archbishop John Quinn, who has a reputation for extending compassion to homosexual persons while condemning the gay lifestyle, invited AIDS patients and ministers of all faiths to participate in a Saturday night mass in which the sick were anointed with oil and prayed for with the "laying on of hands." Six hundred people attended the ceremony and prayed, "Lord Jesus, hear our prayer."

The marathon weekend of prayer and healing, called "Forty Hours of Devotion," was revived from the medieval liturgy first invoked in 1537 in Italy when thousands were dying of the black plague. It was resurrected from obscurity and offered as a sign of hope in a city where forty persons with AIDS (the majority gay) die each month.

Archbishop Quinn also blessed the parish covenant, Most Holy Redeemer Center, where the mass took place, and dedicated it as a home for the terminally ill. Two years later, Coming Home Hospice was opened to persons dying of AIDS.

The AIDS Interfaith Network, which evolved out of the "Forty Hours of Devotion," now sponsors four healing services each month in the city—in the Episcopal, Unitarian Universalist, Metropolitan Community Church, and Pentecostal traditions.

The Episcopal Church has been equally responsive in AIDS ministry. An Episcopal priest who is a friend of our mission group attempted to start an AIDS hospice in his church after members of his congregation died of AIDS. He supplied us with a letter from his bishop, the Right Reverend William Swing, regarding people's fears of "catching" the disease in church.

The pastoral letter circulated in 1984 when AIDS hysteria was very high. The bishop addressed the concern of sharing the Lord's Supper with "potential AIDS carriers." The bishop informed parishioners that there were no reported cases of AIDS being transmitted through saliva and that there was no medical reason to prohibit the use of the common cup. After calling for compassionate response to persons with AIDS, he wrote:

> I beg your pastoral understanding for the AIDS patient who declines to use the common cup because he or she is afraid of contracting a harmful bacteria that might devastate a system devoid of immune powers. I beg your pastoral understanding for the cautious person who now only receives the bread. And I call upon the family not to heighten divisions by making the common cup a political issue. . . . As for me, I intend, when I celebrate, to eat the bread at the beginning of the holy meal, and at the end after everyone has drunk from the chalice, I intend to receive the cup.[9]

The approach of The Episcopal Church and the Roman Catholic Church have been courageous and forthright in both calming fears and promoting compassion in AIDS ministry. Mainline churches, such as The United Methodist Church and the United Church of Christ, have issued compassionate statements encouraging members to embrace and minister to persons with AIDS.

Among the evangelical churches in San Francisco, our mission group learned, only two had started AIDS ministries. One of these churches, the Four Square Church, actively invites persons with AIDS to their church service, welcomes them in worship, and prays for their healing.

The other church, Calvary Chapel, supports one of its pastors, Jim Brooks, in visiting AIDS patients regularly and talking to them about the Lord. We invited Jim one day to our AIDS mission group to discuss his ministry. While some evangelical pastors find San Franciscans somewhat hostile to the gospel, Jim has found a remarkable openness to prayer and friendship evangelism among gay persons with AIDS.

From listening to others and preparing for our own AIDS ministry, our group learned that homophobia (fear of homosexuals) and fear of catching the disease limited our response to the AIDS crisis. What helped us work through the issues was the example of Mother Teresa, who started an AIDS hospice in New York and Washington, D.C., and who offers these words to her volunteers:

> Maybe you are afraid like many have been afraid of leprosy. Many of your families are afraid. The doctors have explained all about AIDS to the Sisters. It is important to go into this work with confidence. There is now a big problem with suicide. Already two men have jumped from a tall building when they found out they had AIDS. If you are afraid, offer that fear to God. Do not force yourself. If you force yourself, you may be more preoccupied with the forcing than with the loving. What I tell the Sisters is, "If you get it, then you will die and go to heaven."[10]

For Mother Teresa, the issue is love and obedience to the call of God, not judgment or fear. "God is speaking to us through this disease," Mother Teresa believes.[11]

Harold Ivan Smith, Executive Director of Tear Catchers, who frequently speaks about AIDS, agrees:

> This is an incredible hour for the church to be the church. People are dying lonely and desperate for eternal hope and care during their last days on earth. The church is in a unique position to minister to them because of our belief in healing (whether physical or eternal), our belief in comforting, and our understanding of grace. Its time to spend less time on judgment and more time on ministry.[12]

If God is speaking to us through this disease, and if it's an incredible hour for the church to be the church, it's not the first time in church history that a plague like AIDS has called for a compassionate response. William Barclay, in his commentary on Philippians, reminds us how the early church engaged in high risk ministry:

> In the days of the Early Church there was an association of men and women called the *parabolani*, the "gamblers." It was their aim and object to visit the prisoners and the sick, especially those who were ill with dangerous and infectious diseases. In A.D. 252 plague broke out in Carthage; the heathen threw out the bodies of their dead, and fled in terror. Cyprian, the Christian bishop, gathered his congregation together and set them to burying the dead and nursing the sick in that plague-stricken city; and by so doing they saved the city, at the risk of their lives, from destruction and desolation.
>
> There should be in the Christian an almost reckless courage which is ready to gamble with its life to serve Christ and to serve men.
>
> The Church always needs the *parabolani*, the gamblers of Christ.[13]

The risk of AIDS will continue to be debated for years to come. But for the Christian, a healthy abandonment to ministry, whatever the risk, is appropriate. Jesus Christ does not call us to a life and mission without risk. Rather, we are called to count the cost of discipleship and risk all for the kingdom.

Starting an AIDS Ministry

Golden Gate Community's AIDS Mission Group met weekly for a year of prayer and discussion before committing to starting a home for persons with AIDS. As we prepared for such a step, a statement by Andrès Tapia served as a processing tool in preparing us for compassionate ministry: "To avoid much pain and confusion, those who want to minister to persons with AIDS should resolve their theology and philosophy about homosexuality before starting."[14]

Systematically, our mission group set out to address the theological issues AIDS evokes, work out a philosophy of ministry that the group could support, and risk passionate commitment to a desired plan of action.

Addressing Theological Issues

AIDS challenges our concepts of mortality, sexuality and human nature. AIDS ministry quickly cuts through pretense and reveals how shallow and vulnerable we really are when challenged to examine our deepest fears.

When we visit a dying patient, we are often confronted with our own mortality. When we touch someone who has AIDS, we may fear catching the disease. When we pray for someone who is dying, we confront the limits of our human compassion and faith and enter into participation with divine compassion and ultimate trust. When we comfort the gay lover of someone who is living with AIDS, we may question whether God condemns all homosexual love.

As a mission group we grappled hardest with the gay issue—what does Scripture teach about the homosexual condition? Is it genetic or acquired, imposed or chosen? Can a homosexual change and become heterosexual? Is sexual monogamy a moral option for a gay person? Is there a place in God's kingdom and the church for the non-celibate homosexual?

Some members of our group make moral distinctions between homosexual lust and homosexual love, between constitutional homosexuality and those with self-chosen sexual preferences. They believe that constitutional homosexuality, though not the norm in creation, is a reality for 5 to 10 percent of the population, and that such persons are not blameworthy. The Bible, they say, is silent on the subject of same-sex, mutually affirming, monogamous relationships. The case can be made that the Old Testament condemns "sodomy" (anal intercourse) in the context of the cultic, dietary, and hygienic laws of ancient Israel to separate the Jews from other cultures (Lev. 18), but such laws were never considered binding by the early Gentile church.

In the New Testament, the kind of immorality Paul specifically condemns is temple prostitution of both male and female varieties, which was common in the ancient world, and homosexual offenders, who like heterosexual offenders abuse and exploit people and behave promiscuously (I Cor. 6:9-11; I Tim. 1:8-11). Yet the apostle withholds moral judgment (as does Jesus) about monogamous homosexual relationships. Sexual morality, they say, should be applied equally to homosexual and heterosexual relationships.

Other members of our group believe with equal conviction that the Bible supports only heterosexual marriage or celibacy and condemns all homosexual activity (Rom. 1:18-32). The homosexual orientation may be a given, but it is not God's intention. Living the gay lifestyle is sinful. God loves all people and has a place for homosexual Christians in his kingdom and in his church, but they must either change their orientation and get married, or control their orientation and practice celibacy to please the Lord (Matt. 19:1-11). Biblical sexuality is expressed best in Genesis, where God created male and female in his image for each other. Homosexuality, which contradicts God's original intention and will, can be forgiven and healed (I Cor. 6:11).

After months of prayer and Bible study, group members remained divided on this issue. Although we did not achieve theological consensus, we did find ecclesiastical unity. On the basis of Ephesians 2:8, we know that we are saved by grace through faith in Jesus Christ. Anyone who professes Christ as Savior should not be excluded from the worship and fellowship of the church. Rich or poor, black or white, male or female, gay or straight—all who are saved are one in Christ Jesus. Personal lifestyle issues, like sexuality and simplicity, as well as ethical and moral choices such as abortion, going to war, smoking, and drinking are best worked out in counseling sessions and support groups in the ongoing life of the church, and not made prerequisites of incorporation into the body of Christ. The church is called to welcome all persons of faith and those searching for faith, including homosexuals and AIDS patients, in the same way that Christ welcomed the outcasts of his day: "Come to me, all you who are weary and burdened, and I will give you rest" (Matt. 11:28-30).

Church in Trouble over Gay Worshipers

A local, evangelical, Southern Baptist church near San Francisco's gay community in the Castro district came under attack by its more conservative denomination for welcoming gay worshipers and accepting homosexual members.

The pastor of this church was accused of "teaching sexual perversion" and was removed from his teaching assignment at the local seminary. The church was reprimanded by its district and cut off from denominational funding.

The controversy arose from the local church's "open door policy" toward homosexuals and the pastor's position on homosexuality. "We have a consensus that the church should be open to anyone who confesses that Jesus Christ is Lord," said the pastor. "We're here to witness the compassionate presence of God. We're not here to judge people."

The pastor insisted that neither he nor his church had a final theological position on homosexuality. "My feeling is," he said, "that Scripture does not condemn all homosexual relationships. I believe that the Bible

209

has an ethic of human relationships that are faithful, loving, life-enhancing, and caring. If a homosexual relationship has those qualities, then I believe the Bible affirms that relationship."

Such a position was in direct contrast with the president of the denomination's declaration that AIDS was God's judgment on homosexuals.

Despite denominational criticism and loss of financial support, the pastor claimed to have remained faithful to his tradition: "I've not betrayed [my Southern Baptist] heritage. I believe in the authority of Scripture. I believe each person stands before God, is able to interpret Scripture and is accountable to God."

The fifty-member church sponsors programs serving neighborhood residents: the elderly, the mentally disabled, Central American refugees, and low-income families.

Good works notwithstanding, the church's position "goes against everything Southern Baptists believe," said one critic. "We ought to bring homosexuals into the church and help them get out of this destructive lifestyle. The consensus of opinion among Southern Baptists is that the Bible teaches [that] homosexuality is wrong."[15]

Developing a Philosophy of Ministry

While it may not be necessary for a mission group to have complete theological agreement, a group must agree on basic principles, policies, and procedures, or its ministry will be chaotic. Developing a philosophy of ministry begins with clarification of group values. It is communicated by a clear mission statement incorporating those values, and is validated by the fruit it bears.

The list of values that the Golden Gate Community AIDS mission group identified in the process of developing a mission statement included the following: trust in divine healing, intercede in prayer, believe in the miracle of love, learn to let go of fear, withhold judgment, offer healing hugs, receive the gifts AIDS patients have to offer, open up your heart and listen, sit and breathe with the one who suffers, adopt those who adopt you, advocate in action, introduce people to Christ.

Taking your list and writing a concise mission statement that embodies the values of the mission group is a challenge. If an AIDS mission group, for example, values renunciation of homosexual sin, clear-cut conversions, and assurance of salvation, that group will develop a mission statement emphasizing the importance of members' having an evangelical discussion of sin, repentance, and faith with every AIDS patient they encounter.

If a mission group values emphasizing God's unconditional love and acceptance, repentance of the heart, and the struggle of faith, that group will develop a mission statement that reflects this more relational agenda.

A mission statement on AIDS ministry that reflects both evangelical and relational values will be structured accordingly. After fifteen months of weekly meetings, the Golden Gate Community AIDS Mission Group, knowing that our philosophy of ministry would continue to evolve, adopted the following mission statement for a year:

> We are committed to a ministry of peace and reconciliation between persons with AIDS and the Christ who loves them, homosexual persons and the church that needs them, and community members with one another.
>
> Toward this aim, we will seek unity among ourselves, pray for persons with AIDS, withhold judgment from those who suffer, listen to those who strug-

gle with faith, open our hearts to those who share, adopt those God gives us, encourage those whom God is drawing, and guide people toward a redeemed life in Jesus Christ.

Specifically, we are called to support those in our own church and mission family who fear or experience AIDS. We will also extend ourselves in God's love to other individuals and families touched by AIDS outside our immediate community who by divine providence cross our path.[16]

A Place in Life and Death

Golden Gate Community was the only "family" that Charles Henry Smith claimed as his own, both in life and in death.

Like many of our social service clients, Chuck was a drug addict and a drifter. He had been married and had two children, but over the years lost touch with them. He had owned a business, but like all else seemed in his life, it was a failure.

Our first contact with Chuck was in the cold winter of 1985 when he came to us homeless, needing emergency shelter. He had been frequently robbed and evicted from hotels, and was unable to manage his life.

After years of street survival and substance abuse, Chuck contracted AIDS. Condemning him for using dirty needles wasn't needed; he knew the results of his lifestyle.

After sleeping for several days under the stairs at the Oak Street House, our social worker, Al Laser, managed to get him admitted to a hospital. For about two months, he and Doris Hogan visited him there every week.

As the three AIDS-related diseases in Chuck's blood, bones, and lungs progressively became acute, it was clear that Chuck was near death.

Chuck made courageous gestures toward reconciliation and completion of his life. He wrote and attempted to contact his former wife and family. He sent his love to friends at the mission. He read the Psalms in the wee hours of the night and prayed and sang with those who came to see him. He struggled with issues of faith and forgiveness, mortality and spirituality.

At joyful moments he found peace with God, himself, and others. At angry moments his disposition dispelled his peace of mind and heart.

At thirty-five years of age, Chuck died. The only family the hospital knew to call was the staff at Oak Street House. We claimed his body and arranged for his funeral.

Officiating at the service, I recounted some of the details and significance of Chuck's life and death. Others shared remembrances of how he struggled to find faith in God, reconcile broken relationships, and complete his life before he died.

There are at least two ways to struggle with difficult issues in life, I pointed out in my sermon: to wrestle like Jacob until you get the answer, or to embrace like Job life's issues and questions and become part of the unfolding process.

Chuck's way was like Job's. The issues of despair and peace, doubt and faith, anger and gratitude, alienation and friendship, were not easily resolved by Chuck. His conversion was not cut-and-dry. Rather, it was a process of coming to terms with life and hoping to be reconciled to God. It was the struggle to hold on to peace found in precious moments, and to resist the temptation to doubt God's forgiveness and to despair. "I love you guys!" were Chuck's last words to those who had faithfully supported him, listened to his story,

*and witnessed to Christ's presence and love. Before he
died, he knew God's love.*

Risking Passionate Involvement

Mission statements are of little value unless they are
implemented, and implementation will not bear fruit
unless the timing is right. In God's time, in God's way,
the fruit of ministry appears.

Fruitfulness cannot be measured accurately by
ministry statistics or program success, but by growth
through passionate involvement in people's lives.
Risking passionate involvement in AIDS ministry
means opening your heart to feel the pain and injustice
of a killer disease that strikes gifted men and women in
the prime of their lives as well as innocent children and
unborn babies. It means enlarging your vision of who
God is, what kind of people God loves and accepts, and
how God ministers to those who cry out for help. It
means "hoping against hope" (Rom. 4:18) for a miracle
of love that will heal a person living with AIDS,
physically as well as spiritually.

Passionate involvement can take many forms.

1. *Praying with and for people with AIDS:* Pastoral
experience reveals that most people, even when they are
not Christians, are willing to be prayed for. They will
pray with those they trust and from whom they sense
genuine love. In the process of prayer, spiritual needs
can be addressed and healing can occur.

2. *Sponsoring spiritual healing services:* If you open
your church doors to the sick and dying, they may be
healed in response to prayers of faith. This may
challenge the church's understanding and practice of
divine healing. As one AIDS minister said, "I used to
believe that telling a person they might live was
instilling false hope. Now I believe that if I expect
people to die, it gives them false despair."

3. *Visiting AIDS patients at home or at the hospital:* Often friends and family abandon a person diagnosed with AIDS. Fear of catching the disease as well as inability to deal with the issues of life and death inhibit most people from extending themselves. This void of emotional and spiritual support that can be filled by caring Christians who are consistent in their support. If you commit to visit and adopt an AIDS patient, you are committing to visit and support that person for the rest of his or her life!

4. *Providing practical help:* When a person is learning to live in the face of terminal illness, even the smallest tasks become a burden. Assisting with cooking, cleaning, shopping, and transportation speaks louder than words. Help with housing, employment, and finances is a living witness of God's love. Assisting incontinent and ambulatory patients requires special training, but can be accomplished in the home.

5. *Supporting caregivers and families of persons with AIDS:* Volunteers burn out, and families of patients grow weary of giving. Even professional health workers have a two year average work span before they need a break. Everyone needs emotional and spiritual support and relief from time to time. Just as Aaron and Hur held up the arms of Moses as he grew weary in Israel's battle against the Amalekites (Exod. 17:12), mission group members may be called to support the caregivers on the frontlines in the battle against AIDS.

6. *Learning the language of compassion:* It is important to minister with sensitivity and appropriate presence. Set aside moral judgments and focus on compassion and healing. Begin with your language: Say "person with AIDS" rather than "AIDS victim." Use the phrase "living with AIDS," which instills hope, rather than "dying with AIDS," which evokes despair. Speak happily when the person being visited is high-spirited, and speak empathetically when the

person is despondent. Respond more to the person's needs and agenda rather than imposing your own. Fulfill the law of love:

> Be joyful in hope, patient in affliction, faithful in prayer. Share with God's people who are in need. Practice hospitality. Bless those who persecute you; bless and do not curse. Rejoice with those who rejoice; mourn with those who mourn. . . . Don't be overcome by evil, but overcome evil with good. (Rom. 12:12-21)

Joey's Family

How do you tell a six-year-old that he has AIDS?

The Caleb family—Joey, David, Larry, and Linda— were adopted by Golden Gate Community's AIDS mission group in 1987. Their situation became the rallying cry for action, calling forth a compassionate response from the whole city of San Francisco.

We met Joey in the summer during a puppet show sponsored by our ministry at the public housing project in the neighborhood where his family lived. As one of the few white children in an otherwise all-black complex, Joey stood out in the crowd. In the fall, we noticed that Joey's complexion had turned pale, signifying sickness. He was taken to the hospital and subjected to six weeks of extensive tests. On October 20, Joey was diagnosed with AIDS.

Members of our mission group met at the hospital to hold a vigil, anoint him with oil, and pray for his healing. Just outside his room, we heard the young child's desperate screams and sobbing questions: "Why are you hurting me? You're hurting my arm!" He had to be sedated in order for the nurses to change his intravenous line.

Once we were allowed in the room, Joey was only semiconscious. Gathered around his bed, we sang and prayed and spoke lovingly to this innocent child for whom the doctors had done all they could. "How could this happen to a six-year-old?" we asked the Lord in shocked silence.

There is no victim more innocent than a baby born premature who received a blood transfusion that six years later proved to have given him AIDS!

The following week Joey was released from the hospital and sent back to the projects. His parents drew straws to determine who would tell him he had AIDS. Linda drew the short one and prayed for wisdom before she spoke.

"Joey, when you were born, the doctors had to give you more blood or you would have died. The blood you were given six years ago contained a disease called AIDS. Nobody knew it at the time, but now we do. AIDS is a disease that some people die from, but not always. All the church people are praying that God will heal you."

When his mother had finished explaining the situation to him, Joey cried.

Circumstances remained discouraging for the Caleb family for several weeks. As Christmas approached, the world celebrated "good news of great joy for all people." But there was no room in the inn for a child with AIDS!

The family was assigned to a tenement apartment that the doctors considered medically unsafe. The neighborhood was high-crime, the housing project drug-infested, and the apartment unsuitable for a child fighting a life-threatening disease.

They suffered through a series of harassments, attempted break-ins, property damage, racial threats, and physical violence. Intravenous drug needles were found on their doorstep, windows were broken out, their truck was set on fire, and the father was physically assaulted.

The frightened family needed to move, and Golden Gate Community did all it could to find a home, but there was no alternative. Other social service and AIDS advocacy agencies were contacted, but they too were unable to locate affordable housing.

We prayed for a clean, safe, and decent apartment where the family could focus on Joey's quality of life. We asked the Lord for a new home for Joey before Christmas Day. We created a ministry fund for "Joey's Home" and solicited sponsors.

Churches took offerings, individuals sent in donations, and social service agencies offered food, clothing, and furniture. The San Francisco Chronicle sent a reporter to interview the family, ran the story on December 23, and pledged to pay the first and last month's rent on any apartment they could afford to rent.

It didn't happen by Christmas, but by New Year's Eve Larry and Linda's deepest prayer was answered— "for Joey to have a home like it's supposed to be, like it's supposed to look and sound and feel."

A small but safe and affordable one-bedroom apartment was located away from the drugs and crime. "And it's clean," said Linda with delight, "and with all the windows, it's very bright!"

The Caleb family began the new year full of hope and the Lord's provisions: Joey, unable to return to school, enrolled in a special class at the hospital. Larry was hired by Golden Gate Ministries job development program and was able to buy a car. Linda brought a material needs list to church and members responded to help make their new home a happy one. The Make-a-Wish Foundation, which specializes in making terminally ill children's dreams come true, sent the whole family to Disneyworld for a special weekend.

For our mission group, Joey's new home was a sign of what is to come—our own ministry home for persons with AIDS.

Where Will We Find Messiah?

The unrelenting question in AIDS ministry is this: Where is God in a world of suffering and injustice? How are the people to know that the Messiah has come?

The story is told in Talmudic literature of a young rabbi asking an older rabbi, "Where will we find Messiah?" The older rabbi responded, "You find Messiah, when he comes, outside the gates of the city changing the bandages of the lepers."

Jesus of Nazareth demonstrated that he was the Messiah by embracing the outcasts and healing the sick with power and authority. "When John heard in prison what Christ was doing, he sent his disciples to ask him, 'Are you the one who was to come, or should we expect someone else?' Jesus replied, 'Go back and report to John what you hear and see: The blind receive sight, the lame walk, those with leprosy are cured, the deaf hear, the dead are raised, and the good news is preached to the poor" (Matt. 11:2-5).

The Gospels record that Jesus healed many lepers in response to willing hearts and simple faith (Matt. 8:1-3). When Jesus was in Bethany, he and his disciples ate in the home of Simon the leper. Jesus was not afraid to "recline at table," the most intimate form of socializing in his time, with someone who had a contagious disease (Mark 14:3).

On another occasion, ten men who had leprosy came to Jesus with a request: "Have mercy on us." All ten were healed. Only one—a Samaritan—is recorded as expressing gratitude. That man came back, threw himself at Jesus' feet, and thanked him (Luke 17:12-19).

219

Jesus' willingness to minister to outcasts and heal many diseased persons was unconditional.

When Jesus commissioned his disciples to go to the outcasts of Israel, he sent them out to "heal the sick, raise the dead, cleanse those who have leprosy, drive out demons. Freely you have received, freely give" (Matt. 10:8).

What better mandate could the church adopt, as the continuing incarnation of Christ in the world, than to embrace the outcasts by our actions?

AIDS is the new leprosy, and the Messiah has come!

Notes

1. *Journal of the American Medical Association*, March 1988, as reported in "AIDS Study Rules Out Saliva and Insects," *San Francisco Examiner*, March 3, 1988.
2. Ibid.
3. Africa has reported the highest number of AIDS cases: 66,000. World Health Organization experts estimate that the true figure is between 100,000 and 150,000 cases. Sharon E. Mumper, "AIDS in Africa," *Christianity Today* 32, no. 6 (April 8, 1988): 36.
4. Centers for Disease Control figures for February 29, 1988. For updated CDC statistics, call the National Sexually Transmitted Diseases Hotline, 800/227-8922.
5. Terry Muck, "The Judgment Mentality," *Christianity Today* 3, no. 5 (March 20, 1987): 16-17.
6. *Surgeon General's Report on AIDS*, United States Department of Health and Human Services.
7. For a full account of the United States government's slow response to the AIDS crisis, see Randy Shilts, *And the Band Played On: Politics, People and the AIDS Epidemic* (New York: St. Martin, 1987).

8. *Surgeon General's Report.*
9. The Right Reverend William Swing, diocese of California, "Pastoral Letter Concerning the Common Cup During AIDS Crisis," pastoral letter of 1984.
10. Quoted by Don McClanen in *The Ministry of Money Newsletter* no. 39 (December 1985): 2.
11. Ibid.
12. Andrès Tapia, "High Risk Ministry," *Christianity Today* 31, no. 11 (August 7, 1987): 16.
13. William Barclay, *The Letters to the Philippians, Colossians, and Thessalonians,* The Daily Study Bible (Philadelphia: Westminster, 1959), pp. 62-63.
14. Tapia, "High Risk Ministry," p. 18.
15. For complete story, see "San Francisco Church in Trouble Over Gay Worshipers," *San Francisco Chronicle,* April 25, 1986.
16. Mission Statement from Golden Gate Community AIDS Mission Group, adopted May 1988.

11

THE INNER GARDEN

Cultivating Contemplation, Community, and Compassion in the City

Without solitude, it is virtually impossible to live a spiritual life. —Henri Nouwen

Here, alone on retreat at Mount Tabor Monastery, in a tiny cell and reflective mood, my head is clear, my heart is warm, and all is well with my soul. Outside my window is a beautiful field of green grass and tulips. The brightly shining sun and the brilliant colors of new spring flowers fill me with desire for my own inner garden to be this peaceful and serene.

I have written this chapter during the season of Lent. I have left the city to embrace solitude out of necessity: I need a time and place to be reflective, to be alone with God, to hear God's voice and rest in eternal love. I need a time and place to deal with my inner thoughts, feelings, temptations, and motivations. I need a time and place to tend to my inner spaces where the Lord walks in the cool of the day.

As an urban minister who seeks to cultivate the spiritual life within, I take seriously Christ's words to his disciples:

> I am the true vine and my Father is the gardener. He cuts off every branch in me that bears no fruit, while every

branch that does bear fruit he trims clean so that it will be even more fruitful. . . . Remain in me, and I will remain in you. No branch can bear fruit by itself; it must remain in the vine. Neither can you bear fruit unless you remain in me. I am the vine; you are the branches. . . . Apart from me you can do nothing. (John 15:1-5)

What must we do to remain in the vine? Who are the branches? How do we bear the fruit of ministry? And where do we find the balance between contemplative spirituality (recognizing the vine), community involvement (recognizing the branches), and compassionate ministry (bearing fruit)?

Contemplation, community, and *compassion* are three essential roots in the garden of God. My purpose here is to celebrate and apply them to urban ministry in the hope that you will also embrace them. In so doing, you will avoid the ministry burn-out that is otherwise inevitable for those who try to take on the city too actively and alone.

Contemplation: I Am the Vine

The garden of God within me is more important than ministry's beck and call. The tree of life in my soul must grow straight and narrow before any mission I have can prosper. Contemplation of Christ as vine is a spiritual discipline requiring daily cultivation of the ground, regular irrigation, and careful pruning. To neglect the inner garden is to dismiss the gift of God's presence. To tend it is to abide with Christ and bear fruit.

Contemplative spirituality does not come easy for me. In honest moments I know myself to be by nature a sinner: unnecessarily active and productive; consumed by my own plans and projects; measuring my worth by my successes and by the opinions of others; manipulating and exploiting others for what seems at the time a good cause; impressed with my own knowledge and insights; and excessively self-interested so as to detract from love for God and neighbor.

In moments of self-honesty and brokenness, God comes to me in love. As I continue examining my temptations and motivations, working through personal life issues, and offering myself to God in quiet devotion, my heart is purified, my life healed, and my friendship with God secure.

I have found that my own need for inner healing and deeper friendship with God is not unique among urban ministers. Dr. Bill Leslie has told in lectures of his own exciting discovery of this essential balance between being and doing, and has allowed me to relate his experience to help others:

When the Well Runs Dry

After twenty years of pastoring the LaSalle Street Church in downtown Chicago, Bill Leslie by his own admission was burned out. "Like an alcoholic who hits rock bottom, I was ready to do something about it," he says about the seriousness of the situation.

Bill had heard of a Roman Catholic nun nearby who had helped a priest who had burned out. He called her for an appointment at the convent and retreat center. Sister Ann listened to Bill for a while and then said, "I want you to find one word that represents how you feel, the first word that comes into your mind."

Bill's word was "RAPE."

"Who raped you?" asked the sister.

"God" is what Bill said, though he was quick to add—"But I don't believe God rapes anybody."

"We're talking about a feeling level," Sister Ann reminded him. "Forget your mind for a minute. The word 'rape' has the connotations of being used and abused. Someone has taken something from you and not given anything back. Now, how has God raped you?"

Bill explained all that he had been through with his congregation over the years, and the feeling that God didn't seem to care or do much to help. "I wanted to resign but I knew I couldn't. God put me in a situation I couldn't handle. I had no resources to do what needed to be done."

"Who else has raped you?" asked the sister.

"The church has!" Bill quickly said. "I have young people and poor people, and they have squeezed me dry like an orange and haven't put a thing back. There's nothing left."

"Well, Bill," said the sister, "let's change the image from that of rape to that of a farm pump. Let's say that everyone who comes by grabs the handle and pumps you."

"That's right," admitted Bill, "and let me tell you how it feels to come home at night. I have four children who meet me at the door and shout 'I want this and I want that!' And when I finally finish with them, it's 10:30, and my wife says to me, "Well, I guess it's leftovers again.""

"So, you feel like you don't have a relationship in the world that doesn't take something from you?"

"I guess so," said Bill, defeated.

"Well, Bill, the problem is not with people working your pump, it's with your pipeline. It's not deep enough. They're pumping you dry by ten in the morning. But if you get your pipe down deep enough into the underground stream, when they pump out water, other cooling and refreshing water comes in. It's what Jesus promised in the Gospel of John: 'Out of your innermost being shall flow rivers of living water.' "

225

Then Sister Ann looked intently at Bill and winked. "I guess what I'm saying is that you need a personal relationship with Jesus Christ."

Bill responded, "Sister Ann, I went to Bob Jones University before I went to Wheaton College. And where I'm coming from, I'm supposed to be saying that to you! But I think I know what you mean."

Sister Ann offered to do spiritual direction with Bill on a monthly basis. She taught him about Christian meditation, contemplative prayer, imaginative Bible study, and other methods of tapping into the inner spring of Christ's presence and strength. In time, Bill's pipeline had found deep water, and when people pumped his handle his well did not run dry.[1]

The reflective, devotional, "being" aspect of Christianity has been called the "journey inward."[2] On this journey we come to know God. We work on the problems with our *pipelines.* We dig down deep into the ground of being and allow the cool, refreshing water of Christ's love to flow freely in. Or, as the prophet Hosea put it, we "break up [our] unplowed ground; for it is time to seek the Lord" (Hos. 10:12).

Contemplation is no easy discipline for active urban Christians. We need the example of Jesus in the desert to remind us of what is foundational for our lives and ministries.

The Desert Experience

After Jesus' baptism and before he began his public ministry, he sought solitude in the desert, that he might pray and spiritually prepare himself for his mission ahead. He was led by the Spirit to the rough and barren hillside south of Jerusalem, where he spent forty days and nights. In the desert wilderness, he was "tempted by

Satan. He was with the wild animals, and angels attended him" (Mark 1:13).

The desert experience for Jesus and for us is one of contemplation, prayer and fasting, struggle and temptation, faith and guidance. These are exercises of the heart discovered only in solitude.

"Solitude is the furnace of transformation," writes Henri Nouwen about the need to be alone with God.[3] "Without solitude," he also says, "it is virtually impossible to live a spiritual life."[4] Father Nouwen, an inspiring, contemplative Roman Catholic priest and seminary professor, counseled me in 1981 as I was preparing to graduate from Yale Divinity School: "Take your sabbatical rest, go to a monastery, embrace a sacred time and place that is just for you and the Lord to be together in silence, before you start your mission in San Francisco."

Going to a monastery was a completely foreign idea to me at the time. Yet after graduating I withdrew to the lonely cornfields of Iowa and entered a Trappist monastery for forty days to experience my own personal desert of preparation for ministry.

In stillness, I found time to simply be in the Lord's presence without having to do anything. I began to experience what it means to "be still, and know that I am God" (Ps. 46:10).

In the absence of noise from the city were the sounds of silence—restless inner voices distracting my contemplation, wild animals disturbing my thoughts, unconscious needs demanding attention. After the first week, I missed my friends, my books, my stereo, and the sounds of city streets. I was not sure I wanted to face my fears and feelings, motivations and temptations, alone in silence.

Slowly, I discerned the still, small voice of God whispering, "Peace be with you," and again, "Fear not, for I have redeemed you; I have called you by name." I

227

began to be attentive to that Voice above all the others. I came to know that God calls me in love by name.

As I increased my times of solitude and listening, I became increasingly aware of the truth that I did not chose God but God chose me, and assigned me the task of starting a church and mission in the city. After surviving in the desert experience, I felt as if the angels of God ministered to me as they did to Jesus in his desert. I emerged with new life and holy purpose, prepared to begin my new work.

Before I left the monastery, I envisioned the Lord "high and lifted up" and myself as God's humble servant. One moment that captured all I experienced that month was my last communion with the monks.

As I took the chalice in my hands to receive, the priest said, "Drink deeply, my son. O taste and see that the Lord is good." I took a sip and felt the wine warming my frame, descending into my being. In that precious moment, I felt like rivers of living water were ready to flood my life and ministry.

Since that summer of 1981, I make it a priority to return once or twice a year to a monastery for a week of prayer and contemplation, in order for my spirit to be renewed. In my active city life, when I get distracted and my motivations get confused, I try to stop what I'm doing and return through prayer and meditation to the inner spring in the garden of God.

Finding the Desert in the City

One does not always have to geographically move to find solitude. The desert of tranquility and transformation can also be found in the city. Sanctuary moments can be created any time, any place. All that is required is a time and place, a focus for solitary prayer, and a willingness to plow up your fallow ground.

Jesus, full of the Spirit, was active in day-to-day

ministry in Galilee. Yet it was his custom to leave the crowd for the garden to be alone with his heavenly father. "Very early in the morning, while it was still dark, Jesus got up, left the house and went off to a solitary place, where he prayed" (Mark 1:35).

Contemplation for Jesus functioned as the way he centered himself in God's will for the day. The practice of Jesus is a pattern for us who would follow in his footsteps. Through daily discipline we can develop a habit of getting up early and creating sacred time and space in our busy daily schedule to be in God's presence. By going into our prayer closets and shutting the door, pouring out our concerns to God, and listening for God's voice, we get centered, and spiritually we prepare for the day.

What helps me keep my commitment to daily prayer and quiet time is a devotional guide. Many are available—some that offer a scripture passage and reflection for each day, and others that provide scriptural themes for the seasons of the church year. I prefer the latter and use *A Guide to Prayer for Ministers and Other Servants* by Rueben P. Job and Norman Shawchuck.[5]

A daily guide plus a weekly reminder in worship about what time it is in the devotional life of the church helps me contemplate the Lord in each season. During Advent, I prepare myself to receive Christ who came to Bethlehem and continues to come into my heart as I make him room. At Christmas I celebrate Christ being born anew within my spirit. During Epiphany, the light of Christ is made known to me in new ways. During Lent, I follow Jesus into the desert of my own inner wasteland to face the areas where I am tempted, and to fast and pray for strength. During Holy Week, I identify with the passion of Christ and face my own mortality and eternal destiny. On Easter, having died with Christ I rise with him in my heart by faith. I celebrate the fact that in him all things are made new! And during the season of Pentecost, I seek a fresh baptism of the gift of the Holy Spirit given to Christ's church for renewed purity and power.

Whether your spirit flows best in the rhythm of the church year or in some other stream, whether your heart is drawn to reading thematic passages of Scripture or to one particular book at a time, what is important is finding a definite time and place to focus on God in silent prayer.

The time can be early morning or late at night. It can last a few minutes or several hours. It can feel "productive" or "empty." But the time must be sacred—set apart and dedicated to holy purpose.

The place can be a mountaintop, a peaceful garden, a prayer closet, or a favorite reading chair. The place you pick to meet with God will become sacred and special if you go there often enough.

The focus for your time with God can be a scripture verse, a selected reading, or a common prayer. But focus we must, or our minds will wander away from God. The only way to deal with distractions is to accept them, but then focus back on that verse of scripture, that sacred word, that line of prayer that calls for our attention. In choosing God over a distraction, we are sometimes caught up in contemplative prayer and a peace that passes human understanding.

Community: "You Are the Branches"

We go to the garden alone, but soon we find that the vine we abide in has many branches. In solitude we contemplate God, but in community we grow in love for God and others. Christianity is a corporate faith, a journey with others in the garden of God.

In the city I experience community on at least two levels: intimately with my family or support group, and corporately in my church or worshiping body.

230

Just as contemplation cultivates unplowed ground, community irrigates dry branches in the garden of the Lord.

Intimate Community

Who are the people in your "soul country"? As a simple journal exercise, draw a circle representing your deepest spiritual self. Put yourself in the center with a dot. Write the names of the few within the circle who are on the journey with you in life and ministry. Add the names of those who are on the border, just outside but occasionally peeking into your soul country. Reflect on this intimate company of pilgrims God has given you as your primary community. Hang onto them for dear life. Love them, nurture them. Invest quality time in their behalf. You won't make it without them!

Rebecca, my incredible wife, is truly my soul friend. She knows me better than any other, is patient with my failings, forgives me when I'm wrong, puts up with me when I'm over-scheduled and preoccupied, balances out my obsessions, and believes in me when others doubt my worth. Most of all she enjoys my company. We belong together. As I said to her on our wedding day, "We are fellow pilgrims on the same road. Let's share life together. You are God's gracious gift to me."

I have two other intimates in my soul country— Chuck Watson in Dallas and Paul Moore in New York. I have known them for ten and fifteen years, respectively, and we have been through much together. Without these and other friends in my life as covenant relationships, I would not be held accountable. I could not get perspective. I would lack confessors outside my daily contacts, and they would lack a counterpart with whom to be completely honest.

Friends for life require commitment, investment of time and energy, and communication. Though distance separates, Chuck and I together with our wives vacation annually. We make it a point to visit, call, and participate in each others' lives. My friend Paul is a co-worker in urban ministry. We keep in monthly contact and retreat together once a year at the same time and place. We use the same *Guide to Prayer* devotional book and are conscious of the shared journey.

Everyone needs companionship—those who know you and love you anyway. No one can develop fully, psychologists tell us, unless one is transparent to at least one other person. The only cure for alienation is a stream of belonging and support flowing through those who dare to love one another.

Beyond your most intimate companions are other members of your core community. Like "soul friends," they keep you honest on the journey and empower you to accomplish your mission.

On the boundary of my soul country, crossing over from time to time, are a number of dear friends with whom I journey. Rebecca's and my support group, for example, is our AIDS mission group consisting of Barry, Bonnie, Steve, Jim, Holly, Muriel, Tami, and Lori. We meet weekly for prayer and sharing, investing in the life we have together. The group is intimate and compatible, a joy to belong to. Whenever we're together I am reminded that I cannot do it alone, but together in Christ, we can do anything!

In community there are opportunities for healing damaged emotions. Only in community can the following disciplines be practiced: bearing one another's burdens (Gal. 6:2); speaking the truth in love (Eph. 4:15); confronting idleness, encouraging timidity, and strengthening weakness (I Thess. 5:14); confessing faults one to another (James 5:16*a*); and praying for one another "that you may be healed" (James 5:16*b*).

Corporate Community

In the New Testament, the word "church" (*ecclesia*) literally means "the called-out ones." We are called out of the world and into community for the sake of worship and mission.

Without the benefits of community, Christianity is a solo experience that leaves one unconnected to the whole. The one who embraces community finds a new identity and a place of belonging. In the process, we overcome our fear of rejection and replace selfishness with sharing; the rough edges of our personalities are rubbed smooth with the oil of gladness, and our bitterness is refreshed by the springs of love. Together we find the strength to be Christ's body in the world.

"How good and pleasant it is when brothers [and sisters] live together in unity!" sings the psalmist about the blessings of community life:

> It is like precious oil poured on the head,
>   running down on the beard,
> running down on Aaron's beard,
>   down upon the collar of his robes.
> It is as if the dew of Hermon
>   were falling on Mount Zion.
> For there the LORD bestows his blessing,
>   even life forevermore.
>
> (Ps. 133:2-3)

It is easy to idealize community life, based perhaps on our perception of the early church in Jerusalem during the first few years after Pentecost. In Acts we read how the first Christians "devoted themselves to the apostles' teaching and to the fellowship, to the breaking of bread and to prayer." We are thrilled about the "wonders and miraculous signs . . . done by the apostles." We romanticize communal life where the "believers were together and had everything in common." And we are challenged by their example of radical stewardship: "Selling their possessions and goods, they gave to anyone as he had need" (Acts 2:42-45).

It only takes a quick look at Paul's letters to the churches to lose idealism. They had conflicts that divided them and besetting sins that tainted them as they learned to love God and live with each other. The idyllic communal practice of the early church in Jerusalem, though noteworthy, did not last the century.

I have witnessed radical stewardship and community accountability in monasteries that have shared resources and practice the disciplines of simplicity, chastity, and obedience. But seldom in the city do such intense communities work. A more practical approach, I believe, is for small groups of Christians to live together or in close proximity, come together regularly for prayer and support, manage their own finances as faithful stewards of the Lord, and give generously to the needs of others. Common meals and shared activities are essential for "life together"—the literal meaning of community.

A community, however large or small, that worships and ministers together is all that really matters ecclesiastically. Church growth, building programs, and denominational obligations pale in comparison to "two or three . . . gathered in my name" (Matt. 18:20 RSV).

What are the essential ingredients of a community of "two or three . . . gathered in my name"? I believe they are these: *solidarity, mutuality, authenticity,* and *commitment.*

When two or more find themselves on a similar path, bonds of solidarity are formed. A "similar path" means sharing a common cause, concern, or vision for worship or ministry. What is shared in common provides the basis for mutuality in the give-and-take of relationships.

Married to solidarity and mutuality are authenticity

234

and commitment. According to Elizabeth O'Conner, authenticity means that when all is said and done the gift we have to give is to be our real selves with one another. "We dip into our own lives and offer what we find there."[6]

Commitment in community means to make a willful choice not to abandon the group. As O'Conner emphasizes, "Certainly within our own small communities we must have a lasting commitment to one another, so that each knows that the other is not going to pull out of the relationship when the going gets rough."[7]

Authenticity and commitment build relationships that mirror our relationship with God. "Community happens," says O'Conner, "when we dare to be naked not only in the presence of God but in the presence of each other, dare to let others see our weaknesses and our strengths, dare to let another hold us accountable."[8]

Golden Gate Community, a worshiping body of about fifty people, began as a house church of five in 1981. We committed ourselves to living together in the same house, enjoyed common meals and fellowship, prayed together daily, and gave ourselves in service to the poor. Daily interaction helped us learn the lessons of the common life.

As others came to be associated with the community, we reevaluated what we were committed to. Community was redefined as *people on a similar path, sharing a common purpose and lifestyle, living together or in close proximity, building relationships for the sake of mission.*

People moved in and out of community relationships during our first two years of journeying together. The original five members dispersed, which brought pain and strife. I learned that community is not paradise. It is hard work for a diverse group of individuals to become a family unit, agree on division of labor and leadership, and work together for a common good without strife and envy. But through faith and perseverance, healing waters can be found in sharing the common life.

By the third year we found our identity as a mission church, devoted to Christ and committed to each other so as to exemplify God's love to the poor. We became a church body with a sacred history and a distinctive kind of worship and ministry.

Today, Golden Gate Community is a city church, attracting worshipers from a variety of backgrounds and persuasions, including rich and poor, young and old, street folks and professionals, ethnics and anglos. Pastored by the Reverend Barry Brown, the church has a vision of planting other worshiping communities and staying tied to mission through Golden Gate Ministries.

In summary, the corporate *community* begins with personal devotion to God and intimacy with a few, leading to a shared journey with a company of pilgrims in an environment where solidarity, mutuality, authenticity and commitment are present.

Mission: "That You Bear Much Fruit"

Jesus taught his disciples that the Gardener, "cuts off every branch in me that bears no fruit, while every branch that does bear fruit he trims clean so that it will be even more fruitful" (John 15:2).

I take this to mean that being a branch in God's vineyard is not enough. We also must bear the fruit of compassionate ministry. Pruning is required because only through our brokenness can we offer healing fruit to others. Compassionate ministry grows out of the Vine. If God is the Vine and we are the branches, we should be broken by the things that break the heart of God. Broken branches can extend compassion to others.

Henri Nouwen, in his book *Compassion*, defines the word "compassion" from its Latin derivatives as "to

236

suffer with." Compassion is a visceral response from the heart that "asks us to go where it hurts, to enter into places of pain, to share in brokenness, fear, confusion, and anguish. Compassion challenges us to cry out with those in misery, to mourn with those who are lonely, to weep with those in tears. Compassion requires us to be weak with the weak, vulnerable with the vulnerable, and powerless with the powerless. Compassion means full immersion in the condition of being human."[9]

Compassion is our *journey outward* in heartfelt service to those who suffer. The reason we walk with God in the garden and commune with others in the cool of the day is so that we can walk with the Lord on the streets of the city in the heat of the night.

In the name of Jesus we feed the hungry, clothe the naked, shelter the homeless, and welcome the stranger. We are the appointed representatives of Christ in the world. As Mother Teresa says, "We do it for Jesus!" Yet compassionate ministry is not simply a matter of doing it *for* Jesus; it is a ministry of our love to him as well. "In the poor it is the hungry Christ we are feeding, it is the naked Christ we are clothing, it is the homeless Christ that we are giving shelter," says Mother Teresa about her vision of the suffering Christ in all who suffer in this life.[10]

Belief in the mystical presence of Christ in all people points to a mystery too deep for words. Perhaps an encounter I had with Mother Teresa will help convey the mystery of compassion.

A Vision That Transforms

The occasion was the thirty-fourth anniversary of the opening of the home for the dying in Calcutta. The sisters and the co-workers were busily moving up and down the rows of stretchers, dishing out food to those who could eat, propping up heads of those too weak to sit up, dressing sores, changing bedpans, and giving lifesaving injections, all in the name of Jesus.

I was there assisting an American nurse who was attending to a young woman very close to death. She had pitting edema, and when I touched her arm a permanent indentation was left. We managed to hook her up to an intravenous line just before Mother Teresa and a priest walked in to announce that an "anniversary mass" would be held in the home in a few minutes.

A medicine table was prepared to serve as the communion table. Mother Teresa gathered us to kneel before the Sacrament. The patients who could sit up in bed did so with great interest and respect.

As mass was said and received, I embraced the sacred moment of Christ's presence. I was kneeling beside Mother Teresa as the elements were passed. To the left of us were a dozen Hindu patients, aware that something life giving was happening in a death home. On the right, a few feet away, was a little alcove where two who had died the previous night lay beneath a sign that read, "I am on my way to heaven."

In that precious moment I experienced the reality of what sustains Mother Teresa—a vision of the suffering Christ both in the appearance of broken bread on a plate and in the appearance of broken bodies on their deathbeds. The appearances were different, but it was the same Christ!

It was a spiritually pregnant moment of kairos—*a sacred time, when the moment is full of deep meaning and divine significance. I was moved and transformed by the experience, having caught a glimpse of what it means to feed on Jesus and to do it unto him as I do it unto the "least of these."*

Reflecting on that experience, I theologized that the resurrected Christ can be discerned in the hearts of those who believe and bear the fruit of Christ in their lives. The suffering Christ can be discerned in the eyes of those who suffer and bear the wounds of Christ in their lives. Every time I look at another human being, I am encouraged by Scripture to look through that person into the face of the resurrected or crucified Christ. Whenever I feed, clothe, or shelter somebody in need, I am encouraged to see through that person to the suffering Christ within. Hence, I feed Christ, I clothe Christ, I shelter Christ, as I help that person in need (see Matt. 25). This is the mystery of compassion, and it is becoming my primary motivation for ministry.

Leaving the Flowers for the Crown

As urban Christians who cultivate the garden of Christ's presence, we must not forget our focus: "Make your home in me, and I will make my home in you. Apart from me you can do nothing." Together, we are broken branches of the vine, which bear good fruit. Contemplation, community, and compassion are rooted and must grow out of the inner garden.

I began this chapter by revealing my reflective, monastic mood. I wish to end it by sharing with you my hike through the woods and my time in the garden. Here at the monastery, a wooded trail begins at the chapel and leads up the mountain to a vista point of inspiring splendor. Along the way there are wildflowers to see and smell, the wind to sense and birds to hear, trees to climb and breathtaking scenes to behold. At the top are some weathered benches encircling a garden. Here I sit in silence, loving God in nature and feeling drawn to the Creator who speaks in the wind and rain, in sunshine and shadows.

After my communion with God in the garden, am I

ready to return to the city? The temptation for me is always to stay in the green garden, walk in the flowery field, and climb the contemplative mountain. Yet I am called to urban ministry, not alone but in community with others, and there is work to be done. I must learn how to walk with the Lord from the garden to the town, from the field of deepening spiritual life to the city where urgent needs are found.

George MacDonald, a nineteenth-century Scottish writer and preacher, offers these challenging words of invitation:

What Christ Said

I said, "Let me walk in the fields."
  He said, "No, walk in the town."
I said, "There are no flowers there."
  He said, "No flowers, but a crown."
I said, "But the skies are black.
  There is nothing but noise and din."
And He wept as He sent me back;
  "There is more," He said; "there is sin."
I said, "But the air is thick,
  And fogs are veiling the sun."
He answered, "Yet souls are sick,
  And souls in the dark undone."
I said, "I shall miss the light,
  And friends will miss me, they say."
He answered, "Choose to-night
  If *I* am to miss you, or they."
I pleaded for time to be given.
  He said, "Is it hard to decide?
It will not seem hard in heaven
  To have followed the steps of your Guide."
I cast one look at the fields,
  Then set my face to the town.
He said, "My child, do you yield?
  Will you leave the flowers for the crown?"
Then into His hand went mine,
  And into my heart came He.
And I walked in a light divine,
  The path I had feared to see.

I left the field and flowers long ago to embrace city life and ministry. I have not yet finished the work or put on the crown. Now and then I go back to sit in the garden, and then again set my face to the town. I find in the active-reflective journey of Jesus a guide for compassionate ministry. If this book has cast some light on the path that leads to peace, then I pray that you who hear the call will "walk in the town."

Notes

1. Bill Leslie has been pastor of LaSalle Street Church in inner-city Chicago since 1961. He speaks often of the need for contemplative spirituality for active ministry.
2. See Elizabeth O'Conner's, *Journey Inward, Journey Outward*, (New York: Harper & Row, 1968).
3. Henri Nouwen, *The Way of the Heart* (New York: Seabury Press, 1981), p. 25.
4. Henri Nouwen, *Making All Things New* (San Francisco: Harper & Row, 1981), p. 69.
5. Nashville: The Upper Room, 1983.
6. Elizabeth O'Conner, *Letters to Scattered Pilgrims* (San Francisco: Harper & Row, 1982), p. vi.
7. Ibid., p. 99.
8. Ibid., p. 104.
9. Donald P. McNeill, Douglas A. Morrison, and Henri J. M. Nouwen, *Compassion: A Reflection on the Christian Life* (Garden City, N.Y.: Doubleday, 1982), p. 4.
10. Mother Teresa, *A Gift for God* (San Francisco: Harper & Row, 1975), p. 39.

APPENDIX

A Guide to Welfare

Many levels of society are subsidized by city, state, or federal government monies. Most "welfare" goes to people who are not poor, through individual and corporate tax breaks, tax shelters, investment incentives, social security, veterans benefits, and farming subsidies. The government also provides some cash and food provisions for those at low-income levels, including poor families with dependent children; people too disabled to work; seniors who worked for years but who are now poor; people who want to work but can't find jobs; people who work hard but don't get paid enough to support themselves.

Many people who qualify for welfare don't know how to tap into these programs. And some who really don't need assistance take advantage of the system. Reforms are necessary, but the current trend toward eliminating programs will wreak havoc on every level. Ideally, the church of Jesus Christ should care for all the needy in the land. Since this is not reality, the state must step in to assist some. Urban missionaries should know what benefits are available, who is entitled to them, and how to advocate for the person in need.

At least nine kinds of government programs are available: (1) food stamps, (2) Supplemental Social Security Income, (3) Aid to Families with Dependent Children, (4) General Relief, (5) Medicaid, (6) Social Security, (7) children's nutritional programs, (8) senior meals, and (9) public housing.

Food Stamps

Almost all stores accept government coupons called food stamps. They may be used only to purchase groceries, not pet food or non-foods like alcohol, tobacco, soap, or paper products. They cannot be used in restaurants. Food stamps are issued to "households"—meaning one person, a family unit, or a group of unrelated folks who live and eat together. "Households" are not required to share expenses except for food. Residents in a group home who receive their meals as part of the program are generally not eligible for food stamps unless they are in an approved drug or alcohol treatment program, federally subsidized housing for seniors, a shelter for battered women, or a group home for the disabled. Residents in a program who must contribute to and cook their own food may be eligible for food stamps.

There are several personal qualifications for receiving food stamps:

1. Members of the eligible household must be United States citizens, legal residents, or refugees who have an indefinite stay of deportation or a voluntary departure date from the Immigration and Naturalization Service and can prove it. An undocumented alien can benefit from living in a household but cannot be included in the food stamp program.

2. Boarders who pay for room and board in your house cannot receive food stamps.

3. Students face stiff rules to qualify for food stamps. Currently, students between the ages of eighteen and sixty who are enrolled at least half-time in higher education, work at least twenty hours per week, and provide more than half the support for another member of their household may be eligible. Failure to meet these requirements results in disqualification of the student and possibly the whole household.

4. Strikers and Supplemental Security Income recipients are usually ineligible for food stamps, although there are some exceptions.

There are at least three income and property limitations for food stamp qualification:

1. The gross-income limit disqualifies households who receive or expect to receive a certain monthly income level (without consideration of taxes, dependent care, working expenses, or high housing costs). In 1987 in California, the gross monthly income eligibility standard for a single household was $507.

2. The net income limit determines how many food stamps a household should get based on income after approved deductions (see current Food Stamp manual for deduction details and other eligibility standards).

3. The resource limit counts cash reserves, stocks and bonds, pleasure vehicles, and property you don't live in or rent out. Resources do not include the house you live in, insurance and pension funds, and personal property being used to generate income, such as tools, rental property, or a work vehicle. Households with more than $1,500 in resources are ineligible for food stamps.

There are employment requirements for receiving food stamps. Those who do not have to work in order to get coupons include (a) those younger than eighteen or older than fifty-nine, (b) disabled persons, (c) eligible students, and (d) participants in an approved alcohol or drug rehabilitation program. Any person in a household who does not fit into one of these categories must apply for work at the State Employment Office if they wish to qualify for food stamps.

There are just two steps in the application process for food stamps: the form and the interview.

A person who believes he or she is eligible for food stamps should contact any county welfare office or phone the federal office (1-800-952-5753) for an application. The county office has thirty days to act on applications they receive. (If a person needs food stamps right away, an "expedited service" may be available.)

An eligibility worker will review the form and conduct a face-to-face interview. The applicant must prove what his or her household's countable income and deductions are, and provide some kind of identification. The eligibility worker will either deny an application in writing or mail the applicant an identification card and notice of approval. The approval document will show the number of months the card is valid and how many food stamps the household will receive. Each month an Authorization to Participate (ATP) card will be mailed to the recipient, which can be exchanged for food stamps at a local outlet. The state law may require a driver's license or Department of Motor Vehicles identification card with a picture on it to get food stamps with the ATP.

Supplemental Security Income

Supplemental Security Income (SSI) is a gold-colored check sent monthly from the Social Security Administration to eligible low-income, aged, blind, or disabled persons. Sometimes SSI provides a person's total income, and in other cases it supplements income received from other sources, up to a maximum amount approved by Congress and the state legislature.

To qualify for SSI, a person must be at least sixty-five years old, have vision testing at 20/200 or worse in the best eye, or be certified "disabled" by a medical doctor approved by the state. To be "disabled" means that a person is unable to engage in substantial, gainful employment because of physical or mental impairments that are expected to last twelve continuous months or end in death.

There are income and property limits for SSI similar to those for food stamps. Those who qualify may also be eligible for state Medicaid programs, homemaker chore services, and payments for "special circumstances" such as essential moving expenses, required housing repairs, unmet shelter needs, and replacement of essential household items lost in a natural disaster.

Applications for SSI are processed at the local Social Security Office, usually within ninety days. An applicant must show proof of age, Social Security number, income, resources, and marital status. General Relief is available to those waiting for their application to be processed.

Applicants who have an alcohol or drug addiction must agree to enter a treatment program if offered, and have a payee (financial manager) administer their checks. Those disabled must agree to accept vocational rehabilitation if offered.

It is difficult for eligible persons to receive SSI payments by their own efforts. They need a patient and persistent advocate. Social workers and mission staff can easily learn the bureaucratic process and offer their services to those who are too old or disabled to help themselves.

Aid to Families with Dependent Children

Aid to Families with Dependent Children (AFDC) provides money to low-income families with children who meet certain qualifications as they move toward supporting themselves.

Benefits are available for (1) children under eighteen living with relatives, (2) single parents who have no regular income, (3) families where both parents are unemployed (less than one hundred hours a month), (4) children in foster care (according to the rules of foster care), and (5) low-income women who are pregnant (once it is verified by a doctor).

The money comes from the state and federal government, but the county runs the program. There are resource and property limits as well as work-incentive requirements to qualify. AFDC families automatically receive medicaid benefits, and in many cases, food stamps and "special need" allowances.

Those with immediate needs can usually receive up to $100 within two days. The normal application process through county social services ("the welfare office") takes from thirty to forty-five days.

Monthly reports are required after a family receives its first check. The purpose is to report whether the family situation has changed or remains the same. Failure to complete the form can result in "adverse action" or discontinuation of payments.

General Relief (or Assistance)

Those who do not qualify for SSI or AFDC may still need financial assistance. Eligibility rules vary from county to county and from state to state, but are designed to identify those who need help most. California has the most generous policy, but most counties in other states offer General Relief to adults at least eighteen years old with no income (definitions vary), few resources (a car and home are allowed), and who are ineligible for other welfare programs.

General Relief usually relates to costs for food, housing, and other basic needs. Some counties give people actual cash and others vouchers for food and lodging. Technically, cash benefits are repayable and a lien can be attached to one's future assets in order to collect, but this rarely happens.

Medicaid

Most states provide free medical care for welfare recipients and other low-income persons. Those receiving SSI and AFDC are automatically eligible for Medicaid. General Relief recipients are no longer automatically eligible but may obtain other forms of medical care from their county health or welfare departments. Low-income persons who are not receiving cash benefits may qualify for Medicaid as "medically indigent."

Recipients must pay the cost of any medical care that is calculated to be "their share," with Medicaid paying the rest. "Their share" may add up to nothing if their income and resources are low enough, or it may be as high as they can afford.

Social Security

So-called "green checks" provide income for workers who are ready to retire. The Social Security Administration provides all the information needed on this gigantic federal program paid by Social Security Tax (FICA) from employees and employers at increasing rates. Social Security provides for four main kinds of insurance benefits: retirement, disability, life insurance, and health benefits (called Medicare).

a. Retirement benefits are paid monthly to the retired worker or the worker's eligible family members. Payments vary depending on how much the worker earned and how many years were covered by Social Security. A minimum of forty quarters or ten years of employment is required to receive payments. Often, this is the only income for growing numbers of seniors and may not be adequate for survival in the 1990s.

b. Disability benefits are paid to workers and eligible family members if a worker is unable to continue working due to a severe, medically certified illness or disability that is expected to last a year or end in death. Newly disabled workers usually start with state disability insurance and then switch to SSI when the state disability runs out.

c. Life insurance benefits are paid monthly to the worker's surviving family members and are based on past earnings. There is a lump sum payment for funeral costs if there is no surviving spouse or entitled child.

d. Medicare is hospital and supplemental medical insurance for Social Security recipients. Premiums are usually charged and the insurance covers up to 80 percent of the medical costs for the elderly.

Children's Nutritional Programs

The federal government has four programs that provide meals to children: (1) School breakfast and (2) school lunch programs are available for schoolchildren whose parents are eligible. (3) The childcare food program is for licensed family day care homes and nonprofit day care centers. (4) The summer food service program provides meals during school vacations at city and county recreation centers and summer camps.

These free or reduced meals are subsidized by the federal government and administered by states and counties. Family size and income qualifications determine whether a family pays full price or reduced price (set by school district) for the meals.

Child nutrition advocates remember when the Reagan Administration in 1981 tried to drastically reduce the standards of the programs. The two-ounce hamburgers with catsup and relish qualifying as the "vegetable" were later upgraded after a public outcry demanded it. Congress has taken steps to ensure that the nutritional programs continue as an investment in the healthy development of the nation's children. Families who are entitled to this assistance should take full advantage of the programs.

Senior Meals

The federal elderly nutrition program provides hot, nutritious meals to persons over sixty years of age who lack sufficient income, ability, or motivation to cook for themselves.

Senior meal centers are usually located in churches, synagogues, or community centers in poorer neighborhoods. Individual contributions are encouraged but not required, and transportation is often provided. There are also senior social services that deliver "meals on wheels" directly to the homes of the homebound. Each locality sets its own rules about when, where, and what to serve; qualifications for delivery; and dietary provisions.

Public Housing

The federal Department of Housing and Urban Development (HUD) provides money to local housing authorities to build and operate public housing projects for low-income people.

To qualify, recipients must be elderly (over sixty-two), physically impaired, or economically disadvantaged. Housing units, commonly called "projects," usually have long waiting lists of applicants. Those who manage to get in are required to pay at least 25 percent of their monthly income for rent. Some projects seek a diversity of low-income, moderate, and higher income levels of tenants in the belief that urban renewal is fostered by interactions between people of various socioeconomic standings.

Another aspect of public housing is providing eligible families with "Section 8 certificates," which guarantee a willing landlord reimbursement by the government for a qualified family's rent.

These nine "welfare" programs are intended to assist persons through a process of transition until they no longer need such support. Unfortunately, what we have seen in this country is the development of a "welfare mentality" and a generational "cycle of poverty" which very few break out of. The church or mission that desires to make a difference must have a staff that understands the programs, can lead needy persons through the system and help them get on their feet again. They also must be willing to advocate for policy changes in the system to ensure economic justice in the land God has given us.

INDEX

LUTHERAN COLLEGE AND SEMINARY

253. 0917
CS54

LINCOLN CHRISTIAN COLLEGE AND SEMINARY

80492